Journal of Biblical Literature
Monograph Series, Volume XII

THE GREEK OF THE GOSPEL OF MARK

by

John Charles Doudna

SOCIETY OF BIBLICAL LITERATURE AND EXEGESIS
224 North Fifteenth Street
Philadelphia 2, Pennsylvania
1 9 6 1

# THE GREEK OF THE GOSPEL OF MARK

Copyright © 1961 by the Society of Biblical Literature
ISBN 1-58983-229-9

All rights reserved. No part of this work may be reproduced or transmitted in any form or by any means, electronic or mechanical, including photocopying and recording, or by means of any information storage or retrieval system, except as may be expressly permitted by the 1976 Copyright Act or in writing from the publisher. Requests for permission should be addressed in writing to the Rights and Permissions Office, Society of Biblical Literature, 825 Houston Mill Road, Atlanta, GA 30329.

Printed in the United States of America
on acid-free paper

CONTENTS

|  | Page |
|---|---|
| Introduction | 1 |

PART I

The Deviation of Mark and the Papyri from the Attic Standard

1. Ellipse of εἰμί : nominal sentences — 4
2. Absence of subject: impersonal verbs — 5
3. Peculiarities in agreement — 8
   A. Verbs with a neuter subject — 8
   B. Lack of agreement in case — 9
   C. The distributive singular — 10
   D. The plural of concrete objects — 10
   E. The plural of abstract expressions — 12
4. Divergences in case usage — 13
   A. Nominative — 13
     1. Use of the nominative to denote extent of time — 13
   B. Vocative
     1. The nominative with the article used for the vocative — 13
   C. Accusative — 14
     1. The use of the dative instead of the accusative with verbs of benefiting and harming — 14
     2. The accusative instead of the dative with verbs of cursing — 15
   D. Genitive — 16
     1. The partitive genitive — 16
        a. Adnominal use — 16
        b. Adverbial use — 17
     2. The genitive with verbs of perception — 18
     3. "    "    "    "    " remembering — 19
     4. "    "    "    "    " separation — 20
     5. "    "    "    " the adjective ἔνοχος — 21
     6. "    "    "    " preposition-adverb εἴσω — 22
     7. "    "    of comparison with ἐπάνω — 22
   E. Dative — 23
     1. The dative with a verb of believing — 23
     2. The dative with passives — 23
     3. The instrumental dative — 23
     4. The dative of specification — 25
5. Prepositions — 26
   A. With one case — 26
     1. εἰς instead of ἐν in a local sense — 26
     2. ἀπό with the genitive instead of a direct object — 27
   B. With two cases — 28
     1. διά with the genitive — 28
        a. διά with χείρ as a periphrasis for the dative — 28

|  |  |
|---|---|
| b. διά with the genitive in expressions of time | 29 |
| C. With three cases | 30 |
| 1. ἐπί with the accusative | 30 |
| a. In the usual sense | 30 |
| b. In extended senses | 31 |
| 2. παρά with the genitive | 32 |
| 3. πρός with the accusative replacing παρά with the dative | 32 |
| 6. Adjectives | 32 |
| A. The use of the positive degree for the comparative | 32 |
| 7. Numerals | 33 |
| A. Peculiarities in the use of εἷς | 33 |
| 1. The use of μία for πρώτη | 33 |
| 2. The use of εἷς for τις | 33 |
| 3. The use of εἷς as a correlative | 34 |
| B. The use of numerals in distributive designations | 35 |
| 8. Pronouns | 36 |
| A. Personal pronouns | 36 |
| 1. Frequency of the oblique cases | 36 |
| 2. The use of οὐ(μὴ)..πᾶς for οὐδείς | 39 |
| 3. Substitute for the pronominal adjective | 39 |
| 9. Verbs | 39 |
| A. Peculiarities in the use of voice | 39 |
| 1. Replacement of the passive by the active | 39 |
| B. Peculiarities in the use of tense | 40 |
| 1. Historical present | 40 |
| 2. Periphrastic conjugation | 42 |
| C. Peculiarities in the use of moods | 47 |
| 1. The optative in subordinate clauses | 47 |
| 2. The absence of an apodosis in a conditional sentence | 49 |
| 3. Substitute for the imperative | 49 |
| 4. The infinitive | 51 |
| a. The infinitive as the complement of certain verbs | 51 |
| 1. With προλαμβάνω | 51 |
| 2. Pleonasm of ἄρχομαι with the infinitive | 51 |
| b. Periphrasis of the infinitive: substitution of πώς for ὡς | 53 |
| c. ἐν with the dative of the articular infinitive | 54 |
| 5. The participle | 55 |
| a. Pleonasm of the participle | 55 |
| b. The genitive absolute | 57 |
| 10. Particles | 59 |
| A. Negations | 59 |
| 1. μή with the participle | 59 |
| 2. Superfluous negatives | 60 |
| B. Conjunctions | 60 |
| 1. ὅτι introductory | 60 |
| 11. Connection of sentences | 61 |
| A. Asyndeton | 61 |
| B. ὅτι recitativum | 61 |
| 12. Prepositions (Pleonasm of) | 62 |

PART II

|  |  |
|---|---|
| Unexplained Markan Usages | 63 |
| 1. The use of ἴδε with a nominal sentence | 63 |
| 2. The exaggerated use of the third plural impersonal verb as a substitute for the passive | 66 |

3. The distributive singular                                              70
4. The use of plurals                                                     73
5. The use of the nominative in time designations                         74
6. The nominative with the article inplace of the vocative                76
7. The dative with πιστεύειν ἐν                                           79
8. The use of the phrase διὰ χειρός as a periphrasis for
     αὐτῷ                                                                 79
9. The use of ἐπί with the accusative as a substitute for
     περί with the genitive                                               81
10. The use of the positive degree of the adjective for the
     comparative                                                          90
11. The use of the cardinal for the ordinal                               92
12. Duplication as a distributive designation                             96
13. The redundant pronoun                                                 98
14. The use of οὐ(μὴ)...πᾶς for οὐδείς                                    105
15. ἔρχεται as equivalent to the passive of φέρειν                        106
16. The periphrasis of the imperfect                                      106
17. The use of εἰ negandi                                                 110
18. Pleonastic ἄρχομαι                                                    111
19. The redundant use of ἀφείς, ἀναστάς and ἐλθών                         117
20. The use of the participle                                             123
21. The use of the phrase ἐν ἐκείναις ταῖς ἡμέραις                        126

Conclusions                                                               128

Statement of the Problem

This study is addressed to the character of the Greek of Mark's gospel: can a place be assigned to it in the development of the koine? If not, how is it to be explained and classified? An attempt is made to compare the degrees and kinds of divergence from the Attic standard in the usages of Mark with those of a body of papyri roughly contemporary with Mark. If both Mark and the papyri depart from the standard of Attic Greek similarly, it may be assumed that both represent the same stage in the development of the koine. If they do not depart from the Attic similarly, how can we account for that fact?

There has been discovered a considerable body of instances which are hereafter to be called 'agreements in difference' or 'agreements in divergence' in which Mark and the papyri share a common departure from the Attic standard. The worth and significance of each of the agreements in divergence must be determined by itself. These items constitute the area common to both papyri and Mark. But there are also a number of divergences in the papyri not paralleled in Mark and some in Mark not discovered in the papyri. The language of Mark and that of the papyri are thus somewhat like two intersecting circles, having an area in common outside of which is an area peculiarly Maran and another peculiar to the papyri. Each of these areas poses its own problems.

a. The area in common: how large is this area and what is its size relative to the single areas? Does it contain essential or incidental agreements? Have these agreements been deflected from the Attic norm by identical influences, or may one assume two contrbuting causes at work separately on the language of Mark and on the language of the papyri, and is this assumption necessary?

b. The area peculiar to Mark: are the items in this area incidental or essential? What hypothesis best explains them? Is non-Semitic or Semitic influence at work?

c. The area peculiar to the papyri: we shall do little more than note the existence of this area. There are in it many usages which are completely outside the scope of the language of Mark and these are not significant for our study.

The language of Mark, then, contains an area of non-agreement with the papyri and one of agreement. What is the relation between the two? Are the items in the area of non-agreement of such weight as to permit the conclusion that there is a language specifically Markan? Can we say that this "language" is a phase of the development of the koine not essentially different from that attested by the papyri? Or is it to be explained on grounds quite apart from those which we know helped to determine the character of the koine?

## Method

The method pursued in this study is as follows: (1) A number of "unclassical" Greek locutions found in Mark is selected. (2) The item of syntax found in each locution will be examined in relation to the usage of classical Greek and to that of the papyri. (3) Attention will next be given to the Markan treatment of the same item noting whether, and to what extent it (a) conforms with Attic usage, (b) agrees with the papyri in differing from Attic, or (c) differs both from the Attic and the usage of the papyri. Each item of syntax will be dealt with in this fashion, and the several areas into which its treatment takes us will be tabulated.

In the second division of our study the cases in which Mark diverges both from the Attic and the papyri are treated with a view to determining what sort of influence is at work on the language of Mark.

To facilitate reference the items of syntax will be treated in the order in which they appear in Blass-Debrunner's grammar.

Part I   The deviation of Mark and the papyri from the
        Attic standard

1. Ellipse of εἰμί nominal sentences

Classical usage in certain circumstances omits some form of the verb εἶναι (AG I, 40ff). Omission occurs in sententious expressions and proverbs; with verbals, expressions of obligation, of necessity, and of time; with adjectives such as ἕτοιμος, δυνατός, οἷος δίκαιος in principal clauses; most commonly in subordinate usage in indirect questions, in constructions with ὅτι and ὡς in protases of conditional sentences, and with a participle when it is equivalent to an adjective and nothing more. Examples of all these are found in the papyri;[1] in addition, the tabular style of official correspondence made for a great number of ellipses of εἶναι : statements about offices or functions, e.g. P. Teb. 29, 1 τοῖς χρηματισταῖς ὧν εἰσαγωγεύς Δοσίθεος (after 110a); partitive designations, expressions of price and the like are all nominal sentences. The following instances of nominal sentence construction in Mark are in accord with classical precedent, as well as with the papyri:

5:9 τί ὄνομά σοι;

6:2 πόθεν τούτῳ ταῦτα, καὶ τίς ἡ σοφία ἡ δοθεῖσα τούτῳ:

9:23 πάντα δυνατα τῷ πιστεύοντι.

34 ...διελέχθησαν ἐν τῇ ὁδῷ τίς μείζων.

50 καλον το ἅλα

10:27 παρα ἀνθρώποις ἀδύνατον, ἀλλ'οὐ παρα θεῷ, πάντα γαρ δυνατα τῷ θεῷ

12:16 τίνος ἡ εἰκων αὕτη και ἡ ἐπιγραφή;

14:19 μήτι ἐγώ;

21 καλον αὐτῷ εἰ οὐκ ἐγεννήθη...

[1] Mayser discusses these and gives examples (GGP II iii, 11-19).

4

36 πάντα δυνατά σοι

The following do not have parallels anywhere except in the New Testament:[1]

1:11  καὶ φωνὴ ἐκ τῶν οὐρανῶν
3:34  ἴδε ἡ μήτηρ μου καὶ οἱ ἀδελφοί μου
5:9   λεγιὼν ὄνομά μοι
7:11  κορβᾶν, ὅ ἐστιν δῶρον, ὃ ἐὰν ἐξ ἐμοῦ ὠφεληθῇς...
11:21 ἴδε ἡ συκῆ ἣν κατηράσω ἐξήρανται
13:1  ἴδε ποταποὶ λίθοι καὶ ποταπαὶ οἰκοδομαί
   7  ἀλλ' οὔπω τὸ τέλος
   8  ἀρχὴ ὠδίνων ταῦτα
  21  ἴδε ὧδε ὁ Χριστός, ἴδε ἐκεῖ...

1:11 is changed by Matthew to the form ἰδοῦ φωνὴ ἐκ τῶν οὐρανῶν λέγουσα by Luke to an indirect construction introduced by ἐγένετο δέ. Although modified by the other evangelists, Mark's form does not seem to be contrary to the usage of the papyri. In view of the form with ἴδε in 3:34, 11:21, 13:1 and 21 we may put a question mark after these passages for consideration later. The ellipse of 5:9 corresponds exactly to the question which it answers and which I have listed above as true to classical usages. The instances in 7:11, 13:7 and 8 are not so far removed from the usage of the Attic as to be considered at all strange. Matthew's parallel to 7:11 is essentially a nominal sentence. 13:7 and 8 are paralleled in other parts of the NT: Heb. 6:8; 1 Cor. 15:21.

2. Absence of Subject (Impersonal Verbs)

The impersonal or indefinite subject in Greek is expressed (AG I,

[1] Cf. Acts 10:15 καὶ φωνὴ πάλιν ἐκ δευτέρου πρὸς αὐτόν -- an exact parallel to 1:11.

36 A. 4):

(a) by τίς;

(b) by the third plural active restricted to matters of common report and opinion, hence with verbs of saying and the like such as φασί, λέγουσιν, ὀνομάζουσιν;

(c) by the third singular passive;

(d) by the second person singular optative or indicative with ἄν.

An exception to classical usage is found in Herodotus ii 106 (ἔρχονται) and in Thucydides vii. 69, line 2 (πάσχουσιν), although the subject in the latter case could probably be gotten from the context.

Examples of (a), (c), and (d) are not mentioned by Mayser (GGP II, iii 3) as occurring in the papyri; (b) occurs with an extension to verbs other than those of hearsay and common report, e.g. P.Teb. 58, 38 γέγραπται ὁ μερισμὸς καὶ δέδωκαν τῶι Μέλανι (the subject evidently is "the ones who supervised the dividing") καὶ ἐπιβέβ(λ:)η(καν) ἡμῖν (σπορoῦ) ἀρτάβας ογβ′    (111a); and P.Ox.744, 4 μὴ ἀγωνιά(σῃ)ς ἐὰν ὅλως εἰσπορεύονται ἐγὼ ἐν Ἀλεξανδρέᾳ μένω    (1a). In the latter example Mayser thinks ὅλως stands for the subject, meaning "(the workers) in a body." These instances do not furnish any decisive proof that the use of the third plural active had gone beyond the classical. But in a papyrus of the second century A.D. is found just such a use, the third plural indefinite for a passive:

BGU 1676, 13 ἐὰν δὲ θελήσῃς μὴ ἀναβῆνε(-ναι) πέμψουσιν στρατιώτην μετ'ἐμοῦ πρὸς σὲ καὶ δίδωμεν (present for future) ἄλλο ἐφόδιον.

In Mark is found an example of (b), several of (c); (a) is present in 4:23 εἴ τις ἔχει ὦτα ἀκούειν ἀκουέτω and is comparable to such as 8:37 τί γὰρ δοῖ ἄνθρωπος ἀντάλλαγμα τῆς ψυχῆς αὐτοῦ; where ἄνθρωπος equals τὶς or a second person singular. As for (c), see 4:24,25 ἐν ᾧ μέτρῳ μετρεῖτε μετρηθήσεται ὑμῖν καὶ προσ-τεθήσεται ὑμῖν. ὃς γὰρ ἔχει δοθήσεται αὐτῷ· καὶ ὃς οὐκ ἔχει καὶ ὃ ἔχει ἀρθήσεται ἀπ'αὐτοῦ also 2:1 ἠκούσθη ὅτι ἐν οἴκῳ ἐστίν. λέγουσιν in 2:18 may be considered an example of (b) since it is not clear just who the questioners are.

There are numerous examples in Mark which agree with the exception to classical usage found in Herodotus (and possibly in Thucydides). In the case of the third plural verbs found in 3:32, 4:38, 5:14, 15, 17, 35 and 6:11 the subjects either are expressed in the manner of that of P.Ox. 744, 4 or are present in the immediate context. There seems to be an impersonal subject for the verbs in the following:

1:32 ἔφερον πρὸς αὐτὸν πάντας τοὺς κακῶς ἔχοντας
2:3 καὶ ἔρχονται φέροντες πρὸς αὐτὸν παραλυτικόν
7:32 καὶ φέρουσιν αὐτῷ κωφὸν καὶ μογιλάλον
8:22 καὶ φέρουσιν αὐτῷ τυφλόν
10:13 καὶ προσέφερον αὐτῷ παιδία
12:13 καὶ ἀποστέλλουσιν πρὸς αὐτόν τινας τῶν Φ.
13:26 καὶ τότε ὄψονται τὸν υἱὸν τοῦ ἀνθρώπου
15:27 καὶ σὺν αὐτῷ σταυροῦσιν δύο λῃστάς

7:32, 12:13, and 13:26 are corrected in Matthew by the insertion of a subject; 10:13, by changing the active to a passive; 15:27, by changing the active to what is a middle or a passive; and 1:32 and 2:3 are not changed. 8:22 has no parallel.

Although we are not treating of passives as such here, a few words about the use of the third person plural impersonal as a replacement for the passive or middle are in order. The instance in 15:27 has a number of such third person plurals preceding it, beginning with οἱ στρατιῶται in 15:16, so that it conceivably could be grouped with 3:32, 4:38, and the rest as having a subject in the context-- at any rate, its significance is lessened considerably thereby. The third person plurals found in 10:34 (not cited above) have an implied subject in τοῖς ἀρχἱερεῦσιν καὶ τοῖς γραμματεῦσιν; however, the chief priests and scribes do not "mock" and "spit" and "scourge" and "kill." Luke has one impersonal third plural in his parallel; Matthew has εἰς with the articular infinitive after παραδώσουσιν. This suggests that we may look upon these third plural impersonals not as a possible use of an active for a passive verb but as instances in which the subject is only vaguely present to the mind of the writer. The verbs in 1:32, 2:3, 7:32, 8:22, 10:13, 12:13 and 13:26 are, however, examples of an impersonal used as a substitute for a passive; Matthew's correction of these (1:32 and 2:3 excepted) shows some distaste for such a practice: there are five corrections and two non-corrections (and in Matthew's gospel itself there are three examples of the use of the third plural impersonal). Luke has three examples of this use; and it is found variously in John, Acts and Revelation. The fact that this usage is limited to the above may be significant; and were it mot for the single example from the papyri, the wide use in Mark and the occurrence in the other three gospels as well as in Acts and Revelation would be extremely significant. As things stand, the practice is not without precedent in the late classical period and parallel in the papyri, but the relatively large number of ex - amples in Mark calls for explanation. Accordingly, the use of the third plural impersonal verb will be further discussed in Part II.

### 3. Peculiarities in Agreement

#### A. Agreement of Verbs with a Neuter Subject

Attention here is directed to the form of the verb, singular or plural, with a neuter subject. That a neuter plural take a singular verb is a rule that is closely observed in Attic Greek (GNTG, section 133). (Homer uses the plural of the verb with a neuter plural subject and instances are found in Plato, Isocrates, Xenophon, Herodotus and Thucydides of a plural used where a number of neuters occur together, each thought of as composing a group or individuality, or where animate subjects are in mind.) The use of the plural for animate objects is observed in the papyri (GGP, II, iii 28f.) with some instances observable of the use of the plural with inanimate objects as in modern Greek:

PSI 1098, 33 ἐὰν δὲ μὴ ἐκποιῶσιν (sc. τὰ ἐκφόρια)   (5Ia)

P.Teb. 20, 7 ἐὰν λογάρια ἀπαιτῶνται   (113a)

And with living objects:

SB 6011 (Ostracon) 5 περὶ τῶν σομάτων (sic)(slaves) τὰ (= ἅ) ἐκεῖ μένουσιν (Ia) (other instances are earlier than the first century B.C.)

Fluctuation in the use of the plural and singular verbs appears in Mark, but in general the trend of the late classical writers and the papyri is followed:

Animate:

1:27  τοῖς πνεύμασιν...καὶ ὑπακούουσιν

3:11  τὰ πνεύματα...προσέπιπτον αὐτῷ

.4:4  καὶ ἦλθεν τὰ πετεινὰ καὶ κατέφαγεν αὐτό

5:13  καὶ ἐξελθόντα τὰ πνεύματα τὰ ἀκάθαρτα εἰσῆλθον

7:28  καὶ τὰ κυνάρια...ἐσθίουσιν

Inanimate:

7:15  ἀλλὰ τὰ ἐκ τοῦ ἀνθρώπου ἐκπορευόμενά ἐστιν

23   πάντα ταῦτα τὰ πονηρὰ ἔσωθεν ἐκπορεύεται

13:4  πότε ταῦτα ἔσται;...ὅταν μέλλῃ ταῦτα συντελεῖσθαι

B. Lack of Agreement in Case

There are two instances in Mark of participles which are not in agreement with nouns, though there is some uncertainty since the nouns with which they agree are not distinctly present. The ὑποδεδεμένους of 6:9 is in a loose relation to the αὐτοῖς of 6:8; this is not so much a palpable grammatical error as it is an awkward construction. σανδάλια is properly all that is needed. The accusative ὑποδεδεμένους agreeing with a possible subject αὐτούς points to an indirect statement after παρήγγειλεν with an infinitive, instead of the ἵνα...αἴρωσιν clause which actually appears. 7:19 has καθαρίζων there is nothing with which it can agree unless it is with "he"(Jesus) understood; RSV, Moffatt, and Goodspeed all take it in this way with the meaning "to pronounce clean." If such is the case then it is Jesus' statement which "makes clean" in contrary emphasis to the statement of the Pharisees that that which goes into the body defiles it. If we take the better attested reading καθαρίζων [1], we may term it a kind of hanging construction.

## C. The Distributive Singular

As far as can be known from consulting the grammar of the classical period and of the papyri, there is no instance of the use of a singular as a distributive designation with a plural subject, e.g. "they were grieved in their heart" (instead of "hearts"), "they shook their head" (instead of "heads"). The instances of such a use of the singular in Mark (3:5, 6:52, 7:21, and 8:17) have parallels in the LXX, and in Luke 1:66, Eph. 6:14, and Rev. 6:11. It has no precedent or contemporary witness that is known in extra-biblical writings. Accordingly it will be one of the items listed for consideration in part II.

## D. The Plural of Concrete Objects

In Attic Greek the plural of concrete objects was employed to denote a particular instance of the generality or to refer to a plurality of the parts which compose the whole of a given classification (AG I, 17 A.1; 18 A.2) e.g. νύκτες meaning the hours of the night, πλοῦτοι the wealth of a particular individual as specific instance of the generality, wealth. From the same way of looking at plurals is derived the

---

[1] It seems doubtful that the text is correct here; καθαρίζων has the better attestation- ℵ ABLW Δ Θ min sa Or- as against the καθαρίζον of KMU al.

use, almost exclusively in poetry (though found also in Plato, Thucydides, and Herodotus), of the plural where but one single object is in mind, viz. ἅρματα where a single chariot is in mind, ἐπιστολαί for one letter, τὰ λύτρα the ransom money. The general classes of this use:

(a) names of festivals and games, such as γάμοι and νυμφεῖα;

(b) names of a few cities, such as Ἀθῆναι, Δελφοί;

(c) οἱ ἥλιοι which is unclassified;

(d) the plural of majesty, from which is derived such an expression as Φρίξου μάχαιραι(Pindar P., 242), meaning "the sword of Phrixus," or θρόνοι "throne" (Soph. Ant. 1041, El. 267);

(e) parts and members of the body;

(f) such miscellaneous expressions as κτενεῖν νιν τοὺς τεκόντας ἦν λόγος (Soph. OR 1176) where the father is meant, τοῖς φυτεύσασιν (OR) 1007) where the mother is meant, πρὸς τοὺς φίλους (Polynices) στείχοντα τῶν ἐχθρῶν κακά (Ant.10), γοναὶ σωμάτων ἐμοὶ φιλτάτων "offspring of the body dearest to me" (Soph.El.1232).

Instances of (a) abound in the papyri (GGP II i 38, 39) e.g. τὰ Σωτηρία Or.gr.36, 5 (276a); Σαραπιήοις(=Σαραπιείοις) P.Teb. I 119, 25 (105-101a). (b) is present in such as Pet. III 46 (5) 2 (IIIa) ἐν Κερκεσούχοις and P.Teb. I 80, 1; 81, 26; 82, 1 (115a) Μαγδώλων. There is no example of (c). (d), the pluralis majestatis, is common but only in the first person. Of (e) there does not seem to be any instance. We find often in the papyri such plurals as ἅλες, τὰ ἔρια, τὰ κρέα, τὰ ξύλα, τὰ ὕδατα meaning the parts which make up a totality, pieces of meat, pieces of wood, bodies of water etc. This is no departure from classical usage (AG I 15, 2), which has such instances as αἵματα (Aesch. Eum. 253), where the blood common to a family or the human race is in mind-- the discrete character of the "bloods" being in the background. The papyri also have a definite class of plurals for designating payments, e.g. τροφεῖα(board), and φόρεθρα, following the model of λύτρα.

In Mark there are instances of (a): 14:1 τὸ πάσχα καὶ τὰ ἄζυμα 6:21 τοῖς γενεσίοις 2:23 ἐν τοῖς σάββασιν Of (b), (c), (d), and (e) there does not seem to be any instance. The plurals in Mark that call for special consideration are the τῶν οὐρανῶν of 1:11, the τοῖς οὐρανοῖς of 12:25 and 13:25, and the ἐν τοῖς δεξιοῖς of 16:5. There are numerous occurrences of the plural of δεξιός in the papyri of which the following are typical:

P.Leid. U=UPZ 81 col.2 τοὺς θεοὺς πάντας παραστάναι(= παρεστάναι) αὐτῆς ἐγ δεξιὸν(=-ῶν) καὶ εὐωμένων(=εὐωνύμον)(IIa)

P.Petr. III 1 (= I 21) col. 2, 21 οὐλη ῥινὶ ἐγ δεξιῶν (237a)

P.Grenf. II 15 col. 1, 12 φακος τραχήλωι ἐγ δεξιῶν (139a)

In the case of οὐρανός as indeed in that of δεξιός <u>one</u> region or area is in mind; it does not, however, fall within any of our classifications and there is no instance of its use in the papyri. It will be further studied in part II.

E. The Plural of Abstract Expressions

The plural of abstract ideas is used to denote specific instances or varieties of the general abstract idea in both Greek and Latin (AG I 17c): στάσεις "acts of sedition," θάνατοι "instances (or kinds) of death." The papyri show the same use (GGP II i, 35, 2). In Mark 7:21 we find πορνεῖαι, κλοπαί, φόνοι, μοιχεῖαι, πλεονεξίαι, πονηρίαι, in which the plural more graphically designates the separate instances of the abstraction.

4. Divergences in Case Usage

A. The Nominative

1. The use of the nominative to denote extent of time

Attic Greek and the papyri use no other case than the accusative to denote extent of time. The nominative is used in Mark 8:2: ἐσπλαγχνίζομαι ἐπὶ τὸν ὄχλον ὅτι ἤδη ἡμέραι τρεῖς προςμένουσίν μοι καὶ οὐκ ἔχουσιν τί φάγωσιν.    B 892 read -αις τρισίν;Δ and the Ferrar group, -ας τρεῖς. Blass-Debrunner see this construction as the result of a mixing of the constructions ἤδη ἡμέρας τρεῖς προσμεν. and ἤδη ἡμέραι τρεῖς (εἰσιν) καὶ προσμεν. They refer to AG II, 418 where ὅσσαι ...νύκτες τε καὶ ἡμέραι practically equal the Latin quotidie, "daily." This hardly does more than suggest a development remotely related to the one under examination. Three other instances are found: Aquila's translation of Josh. 1:11 ἔτι τρεῖς ἡμέραι ὑμεῖς διαβήσεσθε    of Eccl. 2:16 ἤδη αἱ ἡμέραι ἐρχόμεναι τὰ πάντα ἐπεπλήσθη and Acta Pauli et Theclae (so P. Ox. I 63) ἡμέραι γὰρ ἤδη τρεῖς καὶ νύκτες Θέκλα οὐκ ἐγήγερται.     With one exception ἤδη is found in all and is predicative: "Already(are) three days," "already (are) days coming." This strongly suggests a nominal construction from which first the copula was omitted and later the connecting καί. Expressing a time element with an asyndetic verb is a coupling that we shall have to examine further in part II.

B. The Vocative

In classical Greek the vocative case is used where a person is addressed; but the use of the nominative with the article in place of the vocative is not unknown: Blass-Debrunner cite Aristoph. Ran. 521 ὁ παῖς, ἀκολούθει where a subordinate is addressed. As far as we know, there is in Attic Greek no example of a subordinate addressing a superior in this fashion, viz. ὁ θεός for "God." The testimony of the papyri is uncertain.[1]

There are in Mark the following examples of the nominative plus the article replacing the vocative:

5:41 λέγει αὐτῇ· ταλιθὰ κούμ, ὅ ἐστιν μεθερμηνευόμενον· τὸ κοράσιον,...

9:25 λέγων αὐτῷ· τὸ ἄλαλον καὶ κωφὸν πνεῦμα, ἐγὼ ἐπιτάσσω σοι...

15:34 ἐλωΐ, ἐλωΐ, λεμὰ σαβαχθανεί; ὅ ἐστιν μεθερμηνευόμενον, ὁ θεός μου, ὁ θεός μου...

In 5:41 and 15:34 the evangelist by his own statement is translating, so that there is no point in discussing the reason for the presence of the article. The example in 9:25 may well be examined further since it is without precedent in Attic Greek or parallel in the papyri.

C. The Accusative

1. The use of the dative instead of the accusative with verbs of benefiting and harming

Attic usage, in contradistinction to that of other languages, has unvaryingly the accusative with such verbs as βλάπτειν, κακουργεῖν ὠφελεῖν (AG I 295). The papyri, in the main, do not depart from this practice (GGP II ii 298-302), but the uncompounded verbs ποιεῖν and ἐργάζεσθαι with adjectives and adverbs meaning harm or

---

[1] Mayser (GGP II i 55f) adduces a few possible but doubtful examples of the nominative used instead of the vocative and remarks that it is a matter of supposition rather than of established fact:

SB 4013 (Tombstone) Δημήτριος Δημητρίου χρηστὲ χαῖρε (undated)
439 " Καλλιόπη, μήτηρ χρηστή, χαῖρε (Ia)
P.Par. 43 (conclusion) (badly redacted) παραγενομένου (for παραγενοῦ) δὲ εἰς τὴν ἡμέραν (the wedding day) Ἀπολλώνιος
(134a)
P.Leid. C. p.118 2, 7 Ἀπολλώνιος, λαβὲ τοὺς χαλκούς (160a)

In none of the examples, it will be observed, is there any article appearing with the nominative. This replacement of the vocative by the nominative is rare in the papyri.

benefit take the dative (ibid. II ii 263f) as well as the accusative. These datives occur where we would expect accusatives, but with this difference: the person is not so directly affected:

Dative-
P. Grenf. II 36, 11 οὐθὲν ἡμῖν κακὸν ἐπύησεν (=ἐποίησεν) (95a)
Zen. Pap. 59015, 38 φιλικῶς σοι ποιήσομεν (258a)

Accusative-
PSI V 534, 13 ἃ ἐποίησέ με Χάρμος (IIIa)
Zen. Pap. 59361, 31 ἵνα δὲ μὴ κακόν τι ἡμᾶς ἐργάσωνται... (242a)

There is in Mark but one passage for which the foregoing discussion is apposite, and there are three variant readings:

14:7 CDUW syn$^s$ arm- καὶ ὅταν θέλητε δύνασθε αὐτοῖς εὖ ποιῆσαι

A ΧΘΠ have αὐτούς

ℵ BL 892 sa bo have αὐτοῖς πάντοτε

The combined support for the dative, αὐτοῖς or αὐτοῖς πάντοτε is strong. But there is no conflict here with the development of which Grenf. II 36 and Zen. Pap. 59015 are witnesses; hence this may be termed an "agreement in divergence."

## 2. The accusative instead of the dative with verbs of cursing

The dative with καταρᾶσθαι occurs in Attic (AG I 410, 7); the sense is 'pray for adversity upon someone"--not exactly "curse." λοιδορεῖν takes the accusative (ibid. I 294), but the deponent form "to cast reproach upon" takes the dative.

In the papyri such a verb as ἐπιπλήσσω "to scold," "to blame," takes the accusative but ἐπιτιμάω meaning "to cast reproach upon" or "to scold" takes the dative always:

SB 5675 12 τοὺς εἰκῆι ἀνάγοντάς τινας ἐπιπλήσσετε (184-3a)
BGU 1138 22 καὶ αὐτάν) ἐπιπλῆξαι καταξίως (Ia)

P.Petr. II 18 (2) 17 ἐπιτιμῶντος Ἀπολλοδώρωι καὶ Σηράμβωι
(246a)
III 21 (g) 24 τῶν δὲ παρόντων ἐπιτιμώντων σοι
(IIIa)

In Mark there is a verb of cursing taking an accusative:

11:21 ἴδε ἡ συκῆ ἥν κατηράσω ἐξήρανται

Here the act of cursing is crisp and definite; in the papyri and Attic usage the dative seems to be preferred for a milder idea, namely, "objecting to" or "finding fault with," so that the presence of an accusative here is not particularly unusual.

D. The Genitive

1. The partitive genitive

a. Adnominal use

The point to be discussed is the superfluous use of the prepositions ἀπό and ἐκ with the partitive genitive. Classical usage, with the exception of Herodotus and Thucydides, has nothing but the simple genitive (AG I 339) but in the just mentioned authors ἀπό and ἐκ are used with superlatives, number and numerical words, e.g.:

Herod. 1 196 τὴν εὐειδεστάτην ἐκ πασέων

5 87 κεῖνον μοῦνον ἐξ ἁπάντων σωθῆναι

Thuc. 1 110 ὀλίγοι ἀπὸ πολλῶν πορευόμενοι

The papyri exhibit considerable variety in the use of the partitive (GGP II ii 348): ἀπό appears with τὶς, εἷς:

P. Teb. 13, 16 συμφήσαντες ἀπὸ τῶν προγεγρ(αμμένων) ἕνα
(114a)
ἐκ appears, but in general is not as widely used as ἀπό:

P.Teb. 5:56 μηθενὶ ἐξεῖναι λαμβάνειν τι ἐκ τούτων (but in the next line)μηθένα δὲ παραιρεῖσθαι μηθὲν τῶν ἀνιερωμένων τοῖς θεοῖς
(118a)

P.Ryl. II 130...τινες...ἐτρύγησαν ἐκ τῶν καρπῶν οὐκ ὀλίγην ἐλᾶν
(Ip)

And without ἐκ or ἀπό:

P.Teb. II 410 Σωτηρίχῳ̣ἷ̣...χάριν οὗ παρορίζεται ὑπὸ
γίτονος ἐωνημένου τῶν γιτνιωσῶν αὐτῷ (16p)

Mark echoes the fluctuation of the papyri, but seems to be closer to classical precedent. We find:

(a) with τις-

7:2 τινὰς τῶν μαθητῶν

8:3 καί τινες αὐτῶν ἀπὸ μακρόθεν ἥκασιν

12:13 καὶ ἀποστέλλουσιν πρὸς αὐτόν τινας τῶν Φ.

(b) with εἷς-

9:7 καὶ ἀπεκρίθη αὐτῷ εἷς ἐκ τοῦ ὄχλου

14:18 ὅτι εἷς ἐξ ὑμῶν παραδώσει με
    (but compare)
20 εἷς τῶν δώδεκα

(c) with a superlative word-

4:31 μικρότερον ὂν πάντων τῶν σπερμάτων
    (comparative form of adjective for superlative)

There is no departure here from the Attic: the εἷς which appears with ἐκ is in keeping with the examples from Herodotus and Thucydides.

b. Adverbial use

This differs from the adnominal use in that the partitive genitive is used where we would expect an accusative as the object of a transitive verb. Only a part of a whole is concerned and this idea is conveyed by the use of the genitive rather than the accusative. Hence verbs of eating, drinking, taking, giving, bringing, may take a genitive where the object in question is but a part of the total (AG I 345, 355), e.g.

Xen. Anab. I 5, 7 λαβόντας τοῦ βαρβαρικοῦ στρατοῦ

The papyri agree with the classical use (GGP II ii 195), e.g.

Zen. Pap. 59156, 3 καὶ τῶν γλυκυμήλων λαβὲ παρ' Ἑρμαφίλου
    (256a)
except that the periphrases with ἀπό and ἐκ tend to replace the simple genitive (GGP II ii 351):

BGU 1141, 27 ή(=εἰ) ἦν (if it were possible) δάκρυά σοι
γράψειν (ἐ)γεγραφήκειν ἄν ἀπὸ τῶν δακρύων (14a)

The partitive genitive as the object of the verb follows in Mark
classical examples and adheres to the development seen in the papyri:

Verbs of eating and drinking-

7:28 τὰ κυνάρια...ἐσθίουσιν ἀπὸ τῶν ψιχίων

8:4 πόθεν τούτους δυνήσεταί τις ὧδε χορτάσαι ἄρτων

14:23 καὶ ἔπιον ἐξ αὐτοῦ πάντες

25 οὐ μὴ πίω ἐκ τοῦ γενήματος τῆς ἀμπέλου

Verbs of taking (where part of a whole)-

6:43 καὶ ἦραν κλασμάτων...καὶ ἀπὸ τῶν ἰχθύων

12:2 ἵνα παρὰ τῶν γεωργῶν λάβῃ ἀπὸ τῶν καρπῶν τοῦ ἀμπ.

The papyri have examples of the predicate use of the adverbial
partitive genitive with ἀπό and ἐκ:

P.Teb. 61 (b) 291 ἐπερωτώμενον τὸν κωμογραμματέα, τίς
ἐστιν ἀπὸ τῶν ἀναγραφομένων ἐν κληρυχίαι (118-17a)

2. The genitive with verbs of perception

In classical practice verbs of perceiving such as ἀκούειν and
compounds, αἰσθάνεσθαι, πυνθάνεσθαι take the genitive of the person or thing whose voice, tone, or sound is heard and the accusative of the content of the perception (AG I 357). As such it is really another aspect of the partitive. But the distinction between the genitive and the accusative of the thing whose sound is heard "cannot be sharply drawn always" (ibid. 358 A.5). Herodotus has, for example,

2, 114 ἀκούσας τούτων

115 ἀκούσας ταῦτα

In the papyri there is no deviation from Attic precedent for the verb ἀκούειν (GGP II ii 207): the person whose voice is heard is in the genitive; the content which is heard is in the accusative; and the sound or voice, sometimes in the genitive, sometimes in the accusative:

BGU 1007, 11 ἀκούσαντες φωνῆς (243 or 218a)

P. Leid. C (p. 118) cc. I 25 ἀκούσασα τὴν φωνήν (161a)

Mark has one instance of a genitive--whether of the content or of the sound heard is hard to say--with a verb of perception:

14:64 ἠκούσατε τῆς βλασφημίας

The correctness of the use hinges on the meaning of the word βλασφημίας if it means merely impious language with no precise content, then Mark's genitive and Matthew's accusative follow the classical examples cited. If it has the idea of a distinct affront to the dignity of God, then the genitive of Mark is incorrect and Matthew's accusative is proper. Other contexts containing the word yield the sense of a specific act as well as that of abusive language; lacking some more decisive criterion, we cannot tell whether Mark's use agrees with the classical standard or not.

3. The genitive with verbs of remembering

Verbs of reminding and forgetting in Attic take the genitive of the thing and the accusative of the person (AG I 364). Occasionally the accusative of the thing is substituted for the genitive; ἀνα- and ὑπομιμνῄσκειν take the double accusative (to remind someone of something) more frequently than the accusative and the genitive (ibid. I 364 A.12): ἐπιλανθάνεσθαι at times has the accusative of the thing. μιμνῄσκειν in the passive (or middle) sometimes takes the accusative:

Dem. 18, 283 μεμνῆσθαι τοὺς λόγους

Instances in the papyri of verbs of remembering only are scanty, but the genitive of the thing is found (GGP II ii 209), e.g.

P. Bad. 48, 17 μνήσθητι ἡμῶν (126a)

PSI V 502, 2 καλῶς ἂν ποιοῖς μνημονεύων ἡμῶν (257a)

The object or person remembered is sometimes, in keeping with classical precedent (AG 364 A.12), designated by περί τινος:

PSI 412, 8 περὶ οὗ καὶ Αἴγυπτος ἐμνήσθη (111a)

ἐπιλανθάνεσθαι takes both genitive and accusative of the thing (GGP II ii 211, 14).

The accusative of the thing remembered occurs in Mark, where Matthew's parallel has the genitive:

14: 72 καὶ ἀνεμνήσθη ὁ Πέτρος τὸ ῥῆμα

This has no support in the papyri (except by analogy in the case of ἐπιλανθάνεσθαι) but the use of the double accusative with the active of both μιμνῄσκειν and the compound with ἀνά makes it quite probable that the middle ( to remind oneself of something), and the passive as well, took the accusative of the thing. μέμνημαι, for example, which has an accusative in the example taken from Demosthenes, had the present active sense of the Latin meminisse. The LXX generally has the accusative. The genitive, we may say, was the rule, but occasionally the accusative usurped its place. Apparently, then, Mark is justified in using the accusative with a verb of remembering.

4. The genitive with verbs of separation

Verbs of separation take the ablative genitive. Among them is the verb ὑστερεῖν which has the subject of the deficiency in the nominative and the thing in respect of which there is a deficiency in the genitive (AG I 392), e.g.

Dem. 4, 38 ὑστερεῖν τῶν ἔργων

Sometimes a dative is used to designate the thing in which there is a deficiency (AG I 393 A.8). There is no example where the subject is in any other case than the nominative.

In the papyri (GGP II ii 237) there are cases where, along with the usual genitival construction, the thing which one lacks becomes the subject:

Genitive-

Zen. Pap. 59270, 5 ξύλων οὐκ ὑστεροῦσιν  (250a)

Reversed order-

P. Hibeh 65, 29 ἵνα μηθὲν εἰς ἐμὲ ὑστερήσηι  (after 265a)

Reversed construction, with the accusative of the person-

P. Leid. B. 20,26 εἰς τὸ μηθὲν (pap. μηθὴν) τῶν ἀναγκαίων ἡμᾶς ὑστερεῖν  (162a)[1]

There is one locution in Mark in which there is an unclassical use of ὑστερεῖν coinciding with that just seen in the papyri, and so constituting an agreement in divergence of Mark and the papyri:

10:21 ἕν σε ὑστερεῖ

5. The genitive with the adjective ἔνοχος

In Attic usage ἔνοχος takes either the genitive or the dative, usually the latter (AG I 380): the following examples exhibit the genitive only:

Plat. Leg. 915 a τῶν βιαίων ἔνοχος ἔστω

Lys. 14, 5 τολμῶσι γάρ τινες λέγειν, ὡς οὐδεὶς ἔνοχος ἐστι λιποταξίου κτλ.

In the papyri there is no instance of the genitive; only the dative (GGP II ii 149, 39):

Inscr. from Batn-Herit 70, 18 θανάτωι ἔνοχος  (57-56a)

Mark has two examples of ἔνοχος with the genitive:

3:29 ἀλλὰ ἔνοχος ἔσται αἰωνίου ἁμαρτήματος

14:64 οἱ δὲ πάντες κατέκριναν αὐτὸν ἔνοχον εἶναι θανάτου

These do not violate classical precedent but are without contemporary support in the papyri. This is an instance where papyri and Mark diverge from the Attic in a different way (i.e. Mark and the Attic agree; the papyri follow only one of the permissible classical usages; Mark, the other only). The genitive is usual with ἄξιος and ἔνοχος is a word

---

[1] It is possible that ἡμᾶς is the subject of the infinitive, of course.

of like meaning; accordingly, the latter, in taking the genitive, would not seem to call for explanation particularly.

6. The genitive with the preposition-adverb εἴσω

ἔσω (εἴσω) as a preposition can take the accusative or the genitive in Attic usage (Brugmann-Thumb, Griech.Gramm. p 524, 2), viz. δῦναι δόμον Ἄϊδος εἴσω; ἔσω βλεφάρων.

The papyri diverge from the Attic in using ἔσω as an adverb- it is not used as a preposition. Its function accordingly is, as an adverb, to strengthen a preposition (GGP II ii 528),[1] e.g.

Answering the question, Where?-

BGU 1141 33.56 ἔσω ἐν τῆι οἰκίαι　(Ia)

Acta Pauli et Theclae, 25 ἔσω ἐν τῶι μνημονείωι

Answering the question, Whither?-

PSI IV 542, 5 εἰσβιασάμενος ἔσω πρὸς ἡμᾶς　(IIIa)

There are two instances where ἔσω is used in Mark- one in the manner of the papyri:

14:54 ὁ Πέτρος...ἠκολούθησεν αὐτῷ ἕως ἔσω εἰς τὴν αὐλήν

and the other, in which are telescoped the ideas of motion and rest and a genitive is used:

15:16 οἱ δὲ στρατιῶται ἀπήγαγον αὐτὸν ἔσω τῆς αὐλῆς
(into the inner part of the palace)

This genitive with ἔσω is a kind of partitive doing duty for the word for "the inner part" and the preposition εἰς.

7. The genitive of comparison with ἐπάνω

The usual Attic construction in comparison is the comparative form of the adjective, such as πλείων or ἐλάσσων plus the genitive, or ἤ with the case corresponding to that of the first thing compared. In the NT (Mark and Paul) πλείων is replaced by the Hellenistic preposition

---

[1] In this use it appears in Herodotus (i 182): Mayser thinks the preponderant form ἔσω points to Ionic influence.

and adverb ἐπάνω. Examination of the use of ἐπάνω with the genitive in the papyri--it does not occur in classical Greek--shows that it is used in a local sense only, meaning "up above" and as a replacement for ἐπί (GGP II ii 539, 30). In Mark ἐπάνω equals πλείων in one passage:

14:5 πραθῆναι ἐπάνω δηναρίων τριακοσίων

The use here, together with that of 1 Cor. 15:6 ἐπάνω πεντακοσίοις ἀδελφοῖς seems to show that in Mark 14:5 what we really have is a genitive of price, and in 1 Cor. 15:6 a kind of dative of agent. In both cases ἐπάνω is apparently used as an adverb modifying the numeral, which is thus treated as an adjective. As such it does not mark any particular divergence from the usage of the papyri.

E. The Dative

1. The dative with a verb of believing

The one use that calls for special consideration is that in Mark 1:15 of the preposition ἐν and the dative with the verb πιστεύω. There is no parallel to this in the classical period (AG I 410, 7) nor in the papyri (GGP II ii 257, 14). We assign it to the usages to be studied in part II.

2. The dative with passives

The dative with passives of verbs in the fashion of ὑπό with the genitive generally designates the person in whose interest something happens (AG I 422 c), and the idea of agency is in the background, e.g.

Thuc. 1, 51 αἱ Ἀθηναίων νῆες τοῖς Κερκυραίοις οὐκ ἑωρῶντο
("...were not visible to...")

The use is continued in the papyri (GGP II ii 273):

P.Par. 63, 11, 56 ἠβουλόμην ὀφθῆναί σοι κατὰ τὸ ἐπιβάλλον
(165a)

And in Mark: 9:4 καὶ ὤφθη αὐτοῖς Ἠλείας σὺν Μωϋσεῖ

3. The instrumental dative

(a). The dative is used in classical Greek to denote the means or instrument by which an action is effected (AG I 435 B.7) e.g.

Homer ξ (Iliad) 316 ἵμασεν μάστιγι

Xen. Cyr. 4, 3, 18 προνοεῖν ἔξω πάντα τῇ ἀνθρωπίνῃ γνώμῃ ταῖς δὲ χερσὶν ὁπλοφορήσω, διώξομαι δὲ τῷ ἵππῳ, τὸν δ' ἐναντίον ἀνατρέψω τῇ τοῦ ἵππου ῥύμῃ

Soph. Ant. 164 ὑμᾶς δ' ἐγὼ πομποῖσιν...ἔστειλ' ἱκέσθαι

(b). Similar in appearance but essentially different is the use of the dative in a local sense, (" in the midst of" or merely "in") (ibid. I 436 A. 7):

Homer Ω (Odyssey) 38 ἐν πυρὰ καίειν

and

Xen. Cyr. 1, 6, 2 πυρὶ καίειν

(c). With verbs of measuring and punishing there is used the instrumental dative (ibid. I 437, 9):

Herod. 2, 6 ὀργυιῇσι μεμετρήκασι τὴν χώραν

The papyri show no variation from classical examples except that the preposition ἐν comes to be used:[1]

| | |
|---|---|
| P.Par. 11, 10.13 μαχαίραις τύπτοντας | (156a) |
| 12, 15 λέπει με τῆι μαχαίραι | (157a) |
| P.Grenf. I 38, 11 ἔτυπτεν πληγαῖς πλήοσιν | (II-Ia) |
| P. Par. 28, 13 διαλυόμεναι ἐν τῶι λιμῶι | |

and (by the same author)

22, 21 τῶι λιμῶι διαλυθῆναι            (c.160a)

(b). Local

(In the following two examples weapons are regarded as a part of personal accoutrement; hence ἐν)

P.Teb. 48, 19 ἐπελθὼν Λύκος ἐν ὁπλοῖς            (after 113a)

41, 4 Μαρρείους σὺν ἄλλοις πλείοσι ἐν μαχαίραις παραγενομένου            (after 119a)

---

[1] Mayser says that the preposition ἐν with the dative came into use merely to remove ambiguity as to whether the sense was instrumental or not (GGP II ii 357 footnote 3).

(a) and (b) combined. These are examples where there is no question of a means or instrument by which an action is effected; hence they are not instrumental but local:[1]

P.Petr. II 9 (2) 4 ἃ εἶχον ἐν ταῖς χερσὶν ἔργα    (241-35a)

P.Par. 50, 6 εἶδον Πτολεμαῖον ἔχοντα μάχαιραν ἐν τῆι

χερεί (sic)    (159a)

(c). The dative is also used with verbs of measuring and punishing

P. Hib. 74, 1 μέτρησον μέτρωι δοχικῶι    (250a)

In Mark there are instances of the instrumental dative, but none that violate the usage of Attic and the papyri. Instances of (a): 2:8; 3:32; of (b) 1:8; 6:32; 9:29, 49, 50; 11:28; of (c) 4:24, 10:33.

There would seem to be an extension of the local use in 1:23 and 5:2:   ἄνθρωπος ἐν πνεύματι ἀκαθάρτῳ

ἄνθρωπος ἐν πνεύματι ἀκαθάρτῳ

Blass-Debrunner, after discussing a usage that is classical, refer to this as "less classical" (sec. 219, 4). Compare the reading of 3:30: πνεῦμα ἀκάθαρτον ἔχει and Rom. 8:9 where the expressions ἔχει πνεῦμα and ἐστὲ...ἐν πνεύματι are parallel grammatically but the local significance is somewhat to the fore where ἐν is used. Nothing here conflicts with the practice of the papyri: the local sense of ἐν is extended to mean, when used with the dative of the person, 'in the power of...' 'in the possession of...' (GGP II ii 395 41). The manner in which the spirit in Mark 1:23 and 5:2 overrules the action of the deranged person and the fact that in both instances it rather than the man converses with Jesus supports this understanding of ἐν.

4. The dative of specification

A weakened form of the instrumental dative is the dative of speci-

---

[1] Mayser regards these examples as on the borderline between an instrumental and a local use of the dative (II ii 357, 37).

fication or relation. In classical practice, however, the accusative was far more common (AG I 440 12). In the koine the dative has almost completely replaced the accusative in denoting specification (GGP II ii 285).

Mark's use of the dative in preference to the accusative is in keeping with the trend of the koine (although no ratio between the uses is available to determine which is preponderant):

5:22 εἶς τῶν ἀρχισυναγώγων, ὀνόματι Ἰάειρος
7:26 ἡ δὲ γυνὴ ἦν Ἑλληνίς, Συροφοινίκισσα τῷ γένει

5. Prepositions

A. With one case

1. εἰς instead of ἐν in a local sense-

Where in classical usage we would expect ἐν with the dative εἰς with the accusative appears in a pregnant construction, in which an idea of motion is dominant due to the fact that it is generally used with a verb of motion (AG I 543 B), e.g.

O (Odyssey) 275 ἐφάνη λὶς εἰς ὁδόν (the lion has come to the road and is now to be seen on it)

Similarly:

Xen. Anab. 3.4, 13 εἰς τοῦτον τὸν σταθμὸν Τισσαφέρνης ἐπεφ.

The use of εἰς for ἐν in the papyri (GGP II ii 373) shows that the former is used for the probable reason that there is implicit an idea of motion rather than of rest:

P. Leid. U UPZ 81 II 6 πλοῖον παπύρινον προσορμῆσαι εἰς
        Μέμφιν ('rode at anchor in Memphis') (IIa)

But in the following no idea of motion is present:

BGU 1141, 9 οὐδε σὲ γὰρ δοκῶ εἰς ἐνφανιστοῦ τόπον με
        ἔχειν (14a)

P. Fay. 118, 21 βάλλωι ( sc.τὴν κόπρον) ἐξ ἀρούρας εἰς

τὴν Ψεννόφριν (110p)

BGU II 423, 7 κινδινεύσαντος εἰς θάλασσαν (11p)

There are in Mark numerous instances of the confusing of the prepositions εἰς and ἐν:

1:5 καὶ ἐβαπτίζοντο ὑπ' αὐτοῦ ἐν τῷ Ἰορδάνῃ ποταμῷ

9 καὶ ἐβαπτίσθη εἰς τὸν Ἰορδάνην

39 κηρύσσων εἰς τὰς συναγωγάς...

10:10 καὶ εἰς τὴν οἰκίαν...οἱ μαθηταὶ ἐπηρώτων

13:3 καὶ καθημένου αὐτοῦ εἰς τὸ ὄρος 1

In modern Greek εἰς has completely taken the place of ἐν, and the development, supported by few examples, is seen in the earliest phase in the papyri and is attested abundantly in Mark, as indeed in all the gospels with the exception of Matthew. Revelation makes a correct distinction between εἰς and ἐν; the LXX does not. Very early εἰς begins to displace ἐν as is shown by an official protocol of the third century B.C.: SB 7202, 10f προσπέπτωκεν ἡμῖν ἀπῆχθαι αὐτὸν ἐν τῆι (written over εἰς την) ἐν Κροκοδίλων πόλει φυλακῆι (265 or 227a). Instead of the stock phrase ἐν φυλακῆι we have in later usage εἰς. It can hardly be doubted that Mark simply records a later phase in this practice.

2. ἀπό with the direct object signification

While verbs of fearing commonly take a direct object in the accusative, a phrase with ἀπό and the genitive was also possible where used in a local sense, e.g.

Xen. Mem. II 6, 31 φεύγειν ἀπὸ τῆς Σκύλλης

There is little variation from this in the papyri. Mayser has only examples (GGP II ii 306) of the accusative used with verbs of fearing,

---

[1] The use of εἰς found in 14:9 ὅπου ἐὰν κηρυχθῇ τὸ εὐαγγέλιον εἰς τὸν ὅλον κόσμον is in accord with classical precedent (GNT G sec. 206, 4).

and the list of these in Hellenistic usage is large. There is but one example from the papyri which shows an extension from the local use of ἀπό with the genitive in Xenophon:

BGU IV 1079, 23 ὡς ἂν πάντες καὶ σὺ βλέπε σατόν (sic) ἀπὸ τῶν Ἰουδαίων                                                         (41p)

In Mark βλέπω twice takes a periphrase of the genitive with ἀπό for the accusative:

8:15 ὁρᾶτε, βλέπετε ἀπὸ τῆς ζύμης τῶν Φαρισαίων

12:38 βλέπετε ἀπὸ τῶν γραμματέων κτλ.

The usage could well take its cue from what we find in Xenophon.[1] It is strange that the papyri of the last three pre-Christian centuries have no example. Papyrus BGU 1079 is of unknown origin, written by a slave in financial straits- hence the warning, "Have nothing to do with the Jewish userers!" Olsson (Papyrusbriefe, p.88) quotes Wilcken's comment: "This letter is... the oldest attestation to an anti-Semitism of the business world." Undoubtedly, then, the letter comes from a Jewish milieu, or more precisely, an anti-Jewish milieu. What we find in Mark is neither without classical precedent of a kind nor without contemporary attestation, but it is not certain that the custom of using ἀπο' with the genitive in place of the accusative received all its encouragement from influences inside the stream of Hellenistic development.[2]

B. With two cases

1. διά with the genitive

a. διά with χείρ

[1] cf. Hermas, Man. XI 14 φεύγει ἀπ'αὐτοῦ 'he runs away from him'.
[2] Mr. Emrys Evans, in a paper "Case Usage in the Greek of Asia Minor" (Classical Quarterly xv 1907, 28) cites the following: C. and B. ii p.565 (no. 466) ἐὰν δέ τις μὴ φοβηθῇ τούτων τῶν καταρῶν and Pelagia x. 12 (Useher p. 12) μὴ δειλιάσῃς ἀπ'αὐτοῦ and concludes that the usage is a secondary Hebraism.

διά with the genitive as a substitute for ὑπό or the instrumental dative is used to express more definitely the idea that it is by means of a certain thing an action is effected, viz. "we see by means of the eyes" or "with the eyes" (AG I 436 A.7), e.g.

Pl. Theaet. 184 c σκόπει, ἀπόκρισις ποτέρα ὀρθοτέρα, ᾧ ὁρῶμεν, τοῦτο εἶναι ὀφθαλμούς, ἢ δι' οὗ ὁρῶμεν, καὶ ἀκούομεν, ὦτα, ἢ δι' οὗ ἀκούομεν

Xen. Comm. 1. 4, 5 (ὀφθαλμοὺς καὶ ὦτα) δι' ὧν αἰσθάνονται ἕκαστα

The use is extended considerably in the papyri (GGP II ii 354f):

P.Cairo II A Col.1, 16 συνάψαντες ἡμῖν δι' ὅπλων μάχην (123a)

Brit.Mus. Ryl. 381 πέμψαι μοι διά τινος τῶ(ν) φυλάκ(ων) τὸν μεικρόν (40p)

There is one locution in Mark where διά with the genitive is used as a periphrasis for the dative:

6:2 καὶ δυνάμεις τοιαῦται διὰ τῶν χειρῶν αὐτοῦ γίνονται;

Here it appears that not merely does διὰ τῶν χειρῶν stand for ταῖς χερσίν but that the whole phrase διὰ τῶν χειρῶν αὐτοῦ is a periphrasis for αὐτῷ; that it as such replaces a dative of agent otherwise to be expected with a verb having a passive connotation such as γίνονται does here: the works are done by him. As such it is outside the development shown by the examples from the Attic and the papyri and becomes a part of the area peculiar to Mark.

b. διά with the genitive in expressions of time

To use διά with the genitive as a designation of time, meaning 'at the end of a course of' hence 'after,' is permissible in Attic (AG I 482). The use of the same combination in the sense of 'in the course of' or 'during' is unclassical. Of the two uses of temporal διά the latter is the usual one in the papyri (GGP II ii 420):

Zen. Pap. 59218, 24 ὥστε ἡμῖν καθήκειν διὰ τῆς ἑπταμήνου ἅπαξ (254a)

SB 7259, 15 τῶν τε θυσιῶν καὶ σπονδῶν διὰ νυκτὸς καὶ ἡμέρας συντελουμένων (95-4a)

In Mark there is a use of temporal διά which agrees with the papyri in diverging from the classical standard:[1]

14:58 ὅτι ἐγὼ καταλύσω τὸν ναὸν τοῦτον τὸν χειροποίητον διὰ τριῶν ἡμέρων ἄλλον ἀχειροποίητον οἰκοδομήσω

C. With three cases

1. ἐπί with the accusative

a. In the usual sense

In classical practice ἐπί with the accusative was used in the case of motion; ἐπί with the genitive in the case of rest. There is no departure from this save that the pregnant use of εἰς with the accusative in the place of ἐν with the dative is paralleled by the use of ἐπί with the accusative where a dative or a genitive would be expected, due to the fact that the idea of motion is more or less implied (AG I 543 B), e.g. with παρεῖναι:

Xen. Cyr. 3.3, 12 παρεῖναι ἐπὶ τὰς Κυαξάρου θύρας

Thuc. 2, 34 γυναῖκες πάρεισιν ἐπὶ τὸν τάφον

The papyri observe the rules concerning ἐπί and its cases, show no example of the pregnant construction, but exhibit (a) a little fluctuation in the use of the accusative where a genitive would be expected, since rest is denoted; (b) numerous examples of the use of the genitive where the accusative would be expected since motion is denoted (GGP II ii 369, 25):

(a) ἐπί τινα for ἐπί τινος

[1]Possibly this does not diverge from classical usage- the meaning may be 'after' or 'at the end of..'

P.Paris 50, 10ff. γυνὴ καθημένη ἐπὶ φιάθου παιδίον ἔχουσα ἐπὶ τῆς φιάθου, καὶ ἄλλην (sc. ὁρῶ ?)...ἐπ'ἄλλην φίαθον (160a)

Or.gr. 47, 1 [ἔδοξεν] τῆι βουλῆι καὶ τῶι δήμωι [Πτολεμαι έων ἐπὶ δύο ἐκκλησίας (285-47 or 247-21a)

(b) ἐπί τινος for ἐπί τινα

Rosetta stone 45 ἐπιθεῖναι δὲ καὶ ἐπι τοῦ περὶ τὰς βασιλείας τετραγώνου φυλακτήρια (Amulet)(196a)

P.Par. 62, 2, 2 τούτων δὲ τὰ σύμβολα τεθήσεται ἐπὶ τῆς βασιλικῆς τραπέζης (IIai)

P.Tor.I 8, 17 κονίαν καταστρωννύειν ἐπὶ τοῦ δρόμου (116a)

In Mark ἐπί with the accusative in answer to the question "where?" and ἐπί with the genitive in answer to the question "whither?" are in keeping with the examples from the papyri just given and are agreements between Mark and the papyri in diverging from the Attic standard:

(a)

4:38 καὶ ἦν αὐτὸς ἐν τῇ πρυμνῃ ἐπὶ τὸ προσκεφάλαιον καθεύδων

(b)

4:26 ὡς ἄνθρωπος βάλῃ τὸν σπόρον ἐπὶ τῆς γῆς
9:20 καὶ πεσὼν ἐπὶ τῆς γῆς

b. In extended senses

In Mark there are two uses of the accusative with ἐπί for which precedent in Attic and parallel in the papyri are lacking:

6:34 καὶ ἐσπλαγχνίσθη ἐπ'αὐτούς
8:2 σπλαγχνίζομαι ἐπὶ τὸν ὄχλον
9:12 καὶ πῶς γέγραπται ἐπὶ τὸν υἱὸν τοῦ ἀνθρώπου
13 καθὼς γέγραπται ἐπ'αὐτόν
22 σπλαγχνισθεὶς ἐφ'ὑμᾶς

These two must be assigned to the area peculiar to Mark; they may be said to employ the accusative with ἐπί where περί with the genitive would be proper.

2. παρά with the genitive

The phrase οἱ παρ'αὐτοῦ in classical usage could only mean "those who were sent by (or from) him" (AG I 510). In the papyri (GGP II ii 343) it is almost the equivalent of a possessive genitive:

P. Amh. II 35, 13 τοὺς παρ'ἡμῶν γεωργούς ('our h.')(132a)

B.S.A.A. xiv p. 194 ἐπεὶ Ἡρακλείδης ὁ παρ'ἐμοῦ...τετελεύτηκεν καί ἐστιν ἐν ταῖς παρ'ὑμεῖν ( sic ) νεκραῖς
"Since H., my employee, has died in your district etc." (Ia)

Mark is in complete agreement with the papyri in the use of with the genitive:

3:21 καὶ ἀκούσαντες οἱ παρ'αὐτοῦ ἐξῆλθον (his friends)

3. πρός with the accusative replacing παρά with the dative

There is neither in Attic nor in the papyri any instance of the use of πρός with the accusative where rest is denoted (except the pregnant construction with παρεῖναι (AG I 543; GGP II ii 498). However, since εἰμί stands for πάρειμι frequently, and in the examples in Mark εἰμί with πρός means 'be present,' we conclude that the presence of πρός and the accusative with a verb of rest is not out of keeping with the usages of the koine:

6:3 καὶ οὐκ εἰσὶν αἱ ἀδελφαὶ αὐτοῦ ὧδε πρὸς ἡμᾶς

9:19 ἕως πότε πρὸς ὑμᾶς ἔσομαι;

6. Adjectives

A. Use of the positive for the comparative

As far as can be determined neither classical writing nor papyri employ the positive degree of the adjective for the comparative. It seems to be limited to the Synoptics and 1 Clement. In Mark there are three examples:

9:43 καλόν ἐστιν...εἰσελθεῖν...ἢ...ἀπελθεῖς
45 καλόν ἐστιν...εἰσελθεῖν...ἢ...βληθῆναι
47 καλόν ἐστιν...εἰσελθεῖν...ἢ...βληθῆναι

**This usage will be further** examined in part II.

7. Numerals

A. Peculiarities in the use of εἷς

1. The use of μία for πρώτη

The use of a cardinal for an ordinal in the case of μία for πρώτη is limited to the LXX, the Synoptists, Paul, and Revelation. In Mark we have:

16:2 καὶ λίαν πρωῒ τῇ μίᾳ τῶν σαββάτων

This usage will be examined more closely in part II.

2. The use of εἷς for τὶς

εἷς used as a substitute for the indefinite pronoun τὶς is not entirely wanting in classical writings, e.g.

Aristoph. Av. 1292 πέρδιξ μὲν εἷς κάπηλος ὠνομάζετο

In the papyri there are evidences of the weakening of εἷς into an indefinite pronoun:

Zen. Pap. 59024, 1 τῶν ναυτῶν εἷς ἀποστατεῖ (258a)

P.Teb. 230 τραυματίσαντες ἕνα αὐτῶν (IIaf)

Wessely, Stud. Pal. I, 2,2 ἑνὸς τῶν γεωργῶν μου (IIa)

ὁ εἷς instead of τὶς

BGU 1124, 25 ὁ εἷς αὐτῶν Ταυρῖνος (18a)

The examples of εἷς used for τὶς in Mark are not out of keeping with what we have just seen in the papyri:

9:17 καὶ ἀπεκρίθη αὐτῷ εἷς ἐκ τοῦ ὄχλου

10:17 προσδραμὼν εἷς καὶ γονυπετήσας αὐτὸν ἐπηρώτα αὐτόν (Luke τὶς)

14:18 ὅτι εἷς ἐξ ὑμῶν παραδώσει με
20 εἷς τῶν δώδεκα

and-

14:10 Ἰούδας Ἰσκαριώθ, ὁ εἷς τῶν δώδεκα

The statement of 6:15 προφήτης ὡς εἷς τῶν προφήτων is probably to be taken to mean 'a prophet like (any)one of the (well-known group of) prophets,' with εἷς standing for τις.

3. The use of εἷς as a correlative

The subjects of examination are these: the use of εἷς with and without the article in place of ἕτερος and the use of εἷς in place of the correlatives ὁ μέν...ὁ δέ. In Aristotle we find εἷς used in place of ἕτερος

Πολ. Ἀθ. 37, I δύο, ὧν ὁ μὲν εἷς- ὁ δ'ἕτερος

and εἷς with μέν and δέ:

Rhet. II 20 p. 1393 δύο, ἐν μέν...ἐν δέ...

In the papyri εἷς is used for ἕτερος:

Zen. Pap. 59146, 2 χιτῶνας δύο τούτων τὸν ἕνα χειρι-
δωτόν (256a)

P.Par. 51, 18 ἴδον μίαν αὐτῶν (twin sisters) ἐρχομένην (159a)

And εἷς for ὁ μέν (or ὁ δέ):

Wilcken, Chr. 50, 11 ἐπιστόλια δύο, ἓν μέν... ἓν δέ (IIIa)
Mitteis, Chr. 372, V 14 ὁ εἷς... ὁ εἷς (two sons) (IIp)

εἷς without the article occurs in Mark:

15:27 δύο λῃστάς, ἕνα ἐκ δεξιῶν καὶ ἕνα ἐξ εὐωνύμων
αὐτοῦ

Although exact parallels to this use of εἷς as a correlative without the article are lacking, in view of the alternate usages of εἷς and ἕτερος as well as ὁ εἷς...ὁ εἷς for the standard correlative constructions, we can say that Mark's is within Hellenistic usage.

B. The use of numerals in distributive designations

The repetition of a cardinal number for a distributive designation is ordinarily foreign to classical Greek. There are two examples of vulgar usage:

Aesch. Pers. 981 μυρία μυρία πεμπαστάν (= τὸν κατὰ μυρίους ἀριθμοῦντα)

Soph. fr. 191 μίαν μίαν (= κατα μίαν)

Such repetition is almost equally foreign to the papyri except for a curious construction which combines ordinary classical usage with what we find in vulgar quotations such as the above:

P. Ox. 886, 19 ἔρε(αῖρε) κατὰ δύο δύο    (IIIp)

This example is not contemporary with the period when the gospels were written and its value as an independent attestation is diminished, of course.

In Mark, along with correct distributive usage, we find:

6:7 ἤρξατο αὐτοὺς ἀποστέλλειν δύο δύο

This is without parallel in either classical usage or the papyri, and yet it is not characteristic of either and its occurrence is very limited.

The duplication of the cardinal in place of ἀνά or κατά for a distributive designation is of a piece with the repetition of words other than numerals to denote the distributive:

6:39 ἀνακλῖναι πάντας συμπόσια συμπόσια

40 καὶ ἀνέπεσαν πρασιαὶ πρασιαί

Such repetition is limited to Mark, Matthew, Origen, the LXX, and Hermas. Accordingly, we assign the usages of 6:7, 39, and 40 to the area peculiar to Mark.

8. Pronouns

A. Personal Pronouns

1. Frequency of the use of the oblique cases

One of the outstanding features of the Greek of the gospels is the frequency of the oblique cases of the personal pronoun; Mark shares this to a slight degree. In classical use the personal pronoun is inserted only where it is necessary for clearness. In the papyri various redundant pronouns are found: in some the possessive genitive is to the fore; in others, the accusative. "The more vulgar the style, the more prominent are such pronouns" (GGP II i , 63).

Genitive-

Wilcken, Arch. VI 204, 4ff [ἄν] θρωπος ἀπὸ λιβός μου ἐχόμενος μου [ἀν] απίπτι...καὶ ὥσπερ κεκλημ[ένοι] μου ἦσαν οἱ ὀφθαλμοί μου καὶ...ἀνύγωι τοὺς ὀφθαλμούς μου,

11 ὅτι μεταβέβλημα τὴν κοίτην μου

Accusative and oblique cases with prepositions-

14 ὁρῶ σοι αὐτὸν καθιστῶντα αὐτὰς κα᾽ἀγὼ (sic)ἔμπροσθεν αὐτῶν ἐπορευόμην, ἕως καταλάβω αὐτάς, καὶ ἔρχομαι εἰς τὴν ῥύβην (=ῥύμην) μετ᾽αὐτῶν

28 ὤμην με ἐν Ἀλεξανδρήαι με εἶναι

ὄμην (sic) με προσβύτῃ (sic) με λέ[γιν]          (160a)

The insertion of a μου in the salutation of a letter is unnecessary, since the article in such instances stands for the possessive pronoun of the third person:

P. Ox. 744, 1ff Ἰλαρίων ᾳ Ἄλιτι τῆι ἀδελφῆι πλεῖστα χαίρειν καὶ Βεροῦτι τῆι κυρίᾳ μου          (1p)
(The first τῆι has 'his' understood; the μου with the second is out of keeping with the third-person pronoun for which the article stands in the salutation.)

P. Yale 1543, 1f Ἡρᾶς Διοσκόρῳ τῷ πατρί μου πλεῖστα χαίρειν          (II-IIIp)

But the use of the following is correct:

P. Ox. 1293 Θέων [Φιλ] ουμένη τῇ μητρὶ χαίρειν...σέ ὑγιαίνειν σὺν τῷ πατρί μου (117-8p)

BGU 665 Ἐγὼ τῷ πατρί μου γράφω (Ip)

In Mark there are examples of the repetition of the possessive pronoun in the manner of the papyri vernacular:

3:31 καὶ ἔρχεται ἡ μήτηρ αὐτοῦ καὶ οἱ ἀδελφοὶ αὐτοῦ... 32 ἰδοὺ ἡ μήτηρ σου καὶ οἱ ἀδελφοί σου καὶ αἱ ἀδελφαί σου

Somewhat different is the use of the personal pronoun in clauses where it is palpably unnecessary, since another word already supplies the need in the sentence structure. This pleonasm of the pronoun is found (1) where there is already present a noun in the same case and (2) in relative sentences where the relative word makes a pronoun superfluous. Kühner-Gerth (AG II 433f) cite examples of the insertion of pleonastic pronouns in relative sentences where several words intervene between the relative word and the verb that governs it, e.g.

Pl. Phaed. 99, b ὃ δή μοι φαίνονται ψηλαφῶντες οἱ πολλοὶ ὥσπερ ἐν σκότει...ὡς αἴτιον αὐτὸ προσαγορεύειν

Similarly, Kühner-Gerth mention an example from Euripides (Ph. 1596f) where the personal pronoun μου follows an introductory ὅν.

Pleonasm of the pronoun according to (1) is found in the papyri:

P. Ox. 299 Λάμπωνι μυοθηρευτῇ ἔδωκα αὐτῷ διὰ τοῦ ἀραβῶνα (δραχμὰς) η... (Ipf)

And (2):

P. Ox. 117 ἐξ ὧν δώσεις τοῖς παιδίοις σου ἐν ἐξ αὐτῶν (II-IIIp)

P. Ox. 1070, 26 περὶ δὲ τῆς σεαυτῆς ἐπιμελείας καὶ φροντίδος ἀντὶ παντὸς προνόησον μηδενὸς ὧν ἔχομεν αὐτῶν (IIIp)

Examples of (1) in Mark:

6:22 καὶ εἰσελθούσης τῆς θυγατρὸς αὐτῆς τῆς Ἡρωδιάδος[1]
And of (2):

1:7 ὁ ἰσχυρότερός μου...οὗ οὐκ εἰμὶ ἱκανὸς... τὸν ἱμάντα τῶν ὑποδημάτων αὐτοῦ...

7:25 ἀκούσασα γυνὴ περὶ αὐτοῦ ἧς εἶχεν τὸ θυγάτριον αὐτῆς πνεῦμα ἀκάθαρτον ...   1

P. Ox. 117 and 1070 are not contemporary with Mark--otherwise they are not greatly different from what we find in the gospel. It must be admitted that we lack precise parallels containing one feature of the three locutions from Mark, namely, the fact that the redundant possessive pronoun follows its noun immediately.

With the employment of the pleonastic pronoun by Mark we must list some examples of redundant words used in relative sentences:

13:19 θλῖψις, οἵα οὐ γέγονεν τοιαύτη ἀπ'ἀρχῆς κτλ.

9:3 τὰ ἱμάτια... οἷα γναφεὺς ἐπὶ τῆς γῆς οὐ δύναται οὕτως λευκᾶναι...

6:10 ὅπου ἐὰν εἰσέλθητε εἰς οἰκίαν ἐκεῖ μένετε ἕως ἂν εἰσέλθητε ἐκεῖθεν   2

The instances of the pleonastic pronoun have parallels in Luke (parallel to Mark 1:7), Acts, Philemon, Revelation, I Clement, and the LXX. The examples from the papyri as well as from classical writings show that such a usage was not completely foreign to Attic and Hellenistic Greek, yet the scarcity of parallels and the lack of point-to-point correspondence lead us to set this feature of Mark's language

---

[1] The MS attestation for αὐτῆς in 6:22 is not the strongest: although the reading of ℵ B is ordinarily weighty, their αὐτοῦ cannot be regarded as the word which was in the original. Apparently these MSS have reproduced an error made very early. The αὐτῆς of AC would seem to be the correction of a later copyist; it is omitted by fam. 1 (Codex 1 and its allies). Similarly, αὐτῆς in 7:25 does not have the support of ℵ DWΘ and fam. 1.

[2] What is apparently a redundancy may be only a matter of clarity or emphasis.

aside for further study.

## 2. The use of οὐ(μὴ)...πᾶς for οὐδείς

There is one example in Mark:

13:20 οὐκ ἂν ἐσώθη πᾶσα σάρξ

This, too, will be the object of special examination in part II.

## 3. Substitute for the pronominal adjective

As a replacement of ἕκαστος we find the distributive designation εἷς κατὰ εἷς in Mark 14:19 where Matthew has the reinforced form εἷς ἕκαστος. There are in the papyri such combinations as:

P. Hal. 1 223 ἀγορεύων (sic) καθ' ἓν ἕκαστον        (IIIa)

In Zen.Pap. 59224, 2, Edgar claims that in the words αὐτοὶ καταυτοί which occur at the beginning of the line without any connection with what precedes or follows, there is a formation analogous to that found in Mark 14:19. In the Similitudes of Hermas (IX iii 5 and vi 3) κατὰ (καθ') ἕνα λίθον is used in place of ἕκαστον λίθον. In P.Leid. II x 1, 22 ἓν καθ' ἕν is found. εἷς κατὰ εἷς is indeed a vulgarism, but in view of prior and contemporary usage it must have arisen as a fusion of some sort, possibly of εἷς plus the alternate to ἕκαστος, κατὰ (καθ') εἷς.

## 9. Verbs

### A. Peculiarities in the use of voice

#### 1. Replacement of the passive by the active

In Attic Greek a passive is occasionally replaced by the active of a different verb, usually intransitive, construed as the equivalent of a passive. It appears with a preposition, ὑπό, παρά or πρός and a noun denoting the agent (AG I 98, 5). Examples of this usage are:

Pl. Gorg. 519c εὖ παθόντες ὑπ' αὐτῶν

Xen. Comm. 3.4, 1 τραύματα ὑπὸ τῶν πολεμίων τοσαῦτα ἔχω

The usage is followed in the papyri (GGP II i, 90):

P. Par. 23, 12 ἀποθνήσκω ὑπὸ τῆς λύπης (165a)

P. Cair. Zen. 63, 26 διεφώνησαν ὑπὸ τῶν λαῶν χόρτου
δωδεκακισμύριαι ( sc. δέσμαι) (239a)
(διαφωνεῖν means 'to be lost,' hence here it equals 'to be stolen')

In Mark there is an instance of an active intransitive used as a substitute for a passive, according to classical precedent:

5:31 καὶ πολλὰ παθοῦσα ὑπὸ πολλῶν ἰατρῶν

No exact precedent in Attic or papyri is at hand for such a use of an active intransitive for a passive, as in the following:

4:21 ὅτι μήτι ἔρχεται ὁ λύχνος ἵνα κτλ.

22 οὐδὲ ἐγένετο ἀπόκρυφον, ἀλλ' ἵνα ἔλθῃ εἰς φανερόν.

ἔρχεται and ἔλθῃ are used where passives ( τεθῇ, φανερωθῇ ) indicate that such another passive as "is brought" is understood; lacking an example of such a substitution in Greek other than Mark's, we set this aside for consideration later.

## B. Peculiarities in the use of tense

### 1. Historical present

"The historical present is used to a greater extent in Greek than in other related languages, in lively realistic presentation as well as in plain narrative" (AG I 132, 2). It is interspersed with aorists and imperfects, often for the purpose of calling attention to an event with immediately momentous consequences.

The papyri have comparatively little occasion to use the historical present (GGP II i, 131). Since frequency of occurrence rather than the mere fact of occurrence itself is desiderated, the testimony of the papyri to the use of the historical present in comparison with Mark is at most neutral.

According to Hawkins (Hor. Syn., 143ff) there are 151 historical presents in Mark. Such a present is "comparatively rare in Matthew's narrative and extremely rare in Luke's" (ibid. 143). Out of 108 instances in Matthew where a parallel word for one of Mark's historical presents occurred, 80 record a change to some other than a present tense. In these there are 26 cases where some form of εἰπεῖν (which has no present in use) is substituted for λέγει and 5 cases where ἰδού supplied the dramatic quality of the historical present. Out of 94 parallel words in Luke, 84 are in some other than the present tense: of these, 4 have ἰδού and 32 a form of εἰπεῖν. Further, out of 50 parallels in Matthew to Mark's use of the present of λέγειν 26 have one of the forms of εἰπεῖν and 19 retain the present, in 12 instances in the indicative and in 7 in the participle. Out of 46 parallels in Luke to Mark's use of λέγειν in the present, 32 have some form of εἰπεῖν and 7 have λέγειν. The remaining 7 have the aorists of verbs of speaking other than λέγειν and εἰπεῖν. It would seem that as for λέγειν which is used in about half of Mark's instances of the historical present (72 out of the 151), Matthew's and Luke's changes are a matter of preferring the more usual εἰπεῖν hence the significance of the use of the historical present, considered by itself, is not great.

When we consider the presents of verbs other than those of speaking, we find that of 54 parallels in Matthew 44 are changed to some other tense and 10 agree with Mark; out of 48 parallels to such verbs in Luke 45 represent changes, 1 is in agreement, and the remaining 2 are present participles in the genitive absolute. Matthew registers a strong, and Luke an almost complete rejection of the historical present of verbs other than those of speaking.

Mark's preference for the historical present is shown more clearly by a comparison with John's gospel, where 162 instances in 53 pages of the Westcott-Hort text are found, as against 151 in Mark's 41 pages, although the significance of this is diminished when it is recalled that the proportion of narrative in Mark is much higher than in John and hence there is more occasion for its use. Measured by the historical books of the LXX, Mark is approached only by the translator of I Samuel (I Kingdoms) in the frequency of the use of the historical present: on the basis of the comparison of the English texts of I Samuel and Mark, the former is found to be about a third longer but there is the same number of historical presents in both. Mark has the present of ἔρχομαι 24 times; Matthew has it 3, and Luke but once. Of 27 examples in the LXX of the present of this verb 26 are in I Kingdoms.

The frequency of the present of λέγειν is in itself not significant, as we have seen; it seems to be used from individual and stylistic considerations. Of the remaining historical presents about two thirds--all but those of ἔρχομαι--are apparently used for dramatic heightening of interest. Approximately one third (24 of 79 instances) have ἔρχομαι used indifferently: Matthew usually (15 corrections to 5 agreements) and Luke with but one exception correct this. Now λέγειν and ἔρχεσθαι together form nearly two thirds of Mark's historical presents; most of the changes in tense of λέγειν are not corrections, but the degree of unanimity in rejecting the presents of ἔρχεσθαι raises the question: Is this not because it is a vulgarism? As such a vulgarism, it would seem that it is a part of Mark's style.

2. Periphrastic conjugation

A. Classical Greek makes use of a periphrasis of the present, aorist, and perfect participles with εἶναι (AG I, 38, A.3f)

(a) to give more emphasis to the idea in the verb than is supplied by the simple conjugated form. An example:

Soph. OR 970   οὕτω δ' ἂν θανὼν εἴη 'ξ ἐμοῦ

(b) to predicate of the subject a trait, peculiarity, or continuing condition in the fashion of an adjective:

Th. 3.3, 1 ἦσαν γὰρ τεταλαιπωρημένοι ὑπό τε τῆς νόσου καὶ τοῦ πολέμου

Xen. Anab. 4.7, 2 συνεληλυθότες δ'ἦσαν αὐτόσε καὶ ἄνδρες καὶ γυναῖκες

Th. 2.80, 3 ἦσαν δὲ Κορίνθιοι ξυμπροθυμούμενα μάλιστα τοῖς Ἀμπ.

B. There are some cases of εἶναι with a participle in which the verb and an adverbial expression give the main idea, the participle adding another idea which may be rendered independently by a coördinate or relative clause; or in which the copula does not belong with the participle, but with some other idea in the sentence. Examples are:

Th. 2, 12 ἦν γὰρ Περικλέους γνώμη πρότερον νενικηκυῖα
("There was an opinion of Pericles, which had been the accepted one at an earlier time...")

Xen. Oec. 12, 2 πολλῶν ὄντων ἐπιμελείας δεομένων
("Since there are many who stand in need of attention...")

Herod. 3, 76 ἐν τῇ ὁδῷ μέσῃ στείχοντες ἐγίνοντο

C. There are a few examples which seem to point to the employment of an analytic imperfect for the regular conjugated form:

Xen. Anab. 2.3. 13 ἦν ἡ στρατηγία οὐδὲν ἄλλο δυναμένη

Herod. 1.3.12 κρατήσας ἦν τοῖς ὅπλοις (where προσηγάγετο has preceded)

9, 16 ἦν δὲ τὸ δεῖπνον ποιεύμενον ἐν Θήβῃσι [1]

A. (b) Periphrases in the papyri denoting continuing condition

1. With the perfect participle

In the papyri (GGP II i 224f) periphrasis of the pluperfect and and perfect with the perfect participle and the copula in the subjunc-

---

[1] ἦν ποιεύμενον may be regarded as a judicious use of the periphrastic to give added emphasis to ἐν Θήβῃσι.

tive and optative active and middle-passive is regular; and it is to be found, as well, in the third person plural middle and passive of verbs whose stems have consonantal endings. The presence of perfect participle and copula in other forms than these denotes continuing condition:

Active-

P. Hib. 127, 3 [ἐπεὶ οὐκ ὀλί]γον ἀργύριον ἀφηρπηκότες ε ἴ[σιν]   "...hold in possession money gotten by robbery..."(p.250a)

P.Lond. III 897 ἐὰν δὲ μὴ ἦσ⟨θ⟩α εὑρηκώς τινα ὁδόν   (84p)

Middle-passive-

Kanop. Decr. 54 εἰθισμένον ἐστιν   (236a)

Wilcken, Ost. 1256, 7 οὗ ἤμην μεμισθομένος οἴκου   (147-136a)

2. With the present participle

The following denote continuing condition as in classical practice:

P. Hamb. I 27, 18 ἐνοχλού[μενος πρὸ]ς τῶι σπόρωι εἰμί
"I am engrossed in sowing..."   (250a)

P. Teb. I 72, 197 κ'ἂν ἦι (ἠγῆ) ἐν ὑπολόγωι ἀναφερομένη
"...stands in the reckoning..."   (114-13a)

C. Divergences in the papyri from the Attic in the use of periphrases

1. The future perfect

"The future perfect is regularly rendered periphrastically by ἔσομαι   and the perfect participle"(GGP II i 225, 3). In most of the following examples the future perfect, strictly speaking, is not meant: the participle is to all intents and purposes an adjective:

Active

P. Par. 8, 24 ἔσομαι τετευχυῖα   (129a)

PSI 635, 13 ἔσει εὐεργετηκώς   (IIIa)

P. Lond. I 23 ἔσομαι δι'ὑμᾶς ἐσχηκως τὸν βίον   (158a)

Middle

P. Ox. 1061, 20 ἔσῃ μοι κεχαρισμένος (22a)

BGU 596, 12 τοῦτο οὖν ποιήσας ἔσῃ μοι μεγάλην χάριταν

κατ[α]τεθειμ[έ]νο(ς) (84p)

Passive

SB 5219 (Asylie-Inscr.) 24 ἔσομαι εὐεργετημένος (69-8a)

P. Grenf. I 15, 9 ἐσόμεθα διὰ σὲ βεβοηθημένοι (146-35a)

2. There are in the papyri some cases where periphrases, contrary to classical usage, do not designate continuing condition but are simply substitutes for the regularly inflected form of the verb:

Perfect participle

SB 7267, 3 πῶς ἐστι κεκρατηκὼς ὁ Θώραξ;
"how did Th. come to power?" (226a)

BGU IV 1141, 45 ἔλεγεν ὑφεστακώς μοι ἦν ὁ Διόδωρος

φιλάνθρωπον δοῦναι "D. promised me.." (13a)

Present participle

P. Par. 50, 12 καθῆμεν ἦν καὶ οὐ κινοῦσα (159a)[1]

There are in Mark many instances of εἶναι with a participle; these will be grouped according to the classification used with the papyri and Attic.

A. (b) Periphrases in Mark denoting continuing condition

6:52 ἀλλ' ἦν αὐτῶν ἡ καρδία πεπωρωμένη

15:26 καὶ ἦν ἡ ἐπιγραφή...ἐπιγεγραμμένη

B. There are other cases where, as we stated before (p. 43), "the verb and an adverbial expression give the main idea, the participle adding another idea which may be rendered independently by a coördinate or relative clause." These as well are not contrary to classical usage:

1:13 καὶ ἦν ἐν τῇ ἐρήμῳ τεσσαράκοντα ἡμέρας πειαζό-

μενος ὑπὸ τοῦ σατανᾶ

---

[1] This may simply denote continuing condition; from the verb it is hard to say which of the two (substitute for the imperfect or continuing condition) is the case.

4:38 ἦν αὐτὸς ἐν τῇ πρύμνῃ ἐπὶ τὸ προσκεφάλαιον καθεύδων         "he was in the stern...asleep..."

5:5 καὶ ἐν τοῖς ὄρεσιν ἦν κράζων καὶ κατακόπτων ἑαυτόν

11 ἦν δὲ ἐκεῖ πρὸς τῷ ὄρει ἀγέλη χοίρων μεγάλη βοσκομένη

9:7 καὶ ἐγένετο νεφέλη ἐπισκιάζουσα αὐτοῖς

15:40 ἦσαν δὲ καὶ γυναῖκες ἀπὸ μακρόθεν θεωροῦσαι

C. Finally, there are a number of periphrases for the imperfect and the future for which there is no clear example in Attic Greek and little attestation in the papyri:[1]

2:6 ἦσαν δέ τινες τῶν γραμματέων ἐκεῖ καθήμενοι καὶ διαλογιζόμενοι         (Matt. εἶπον, Luke ἤρξαντο διαλογίζεσθαι)

18 ἦσαν οἱ μαθηταὶ Ἰωάννου καὶ οἱ Φαρισαῖοι νηστεύοντες

9:4 καὶ ἦσαν συνλαλοῦντες τῷ Ἰησοῦ (Matt., participle only)

10:22 ἦν γὰρ ἔχων κτήματα πολλά         [2]

32 ἦσαν δὲ ἐν τῇ ὁδῷ ἀναβαίνοντες εἰς Ἰ.
        (Matt., present participle with παρέλαβεν)
        καὶ ἦν προάγων αὐτοὺς ὁ Ἰησοῦς

13:25 καὶ οἱ ἀστέρες ἔσονται ἐκ τοῦ οὐρανοῦ πίπτοντες
        (Matt., πεσοῦνται)

14:4 ἦσαν δέ τινες ἀγανακτοῦντες πρὸς ἑαυτούς
        (Matt., ἠγανάκτησον)

54 καὶ ἦν συνκαθήμενος    (Matt. and Luke, ἐκάθητο)

15:43 καὶ αὐτὸς ἦν προσδεχόμενος τὴν βασιλείαν τοῦ θεοῦ

---

[1] For the periphrastic future perfect and perfect in the papyri--which constitute divergences from the Attic standard--there is nothing in Mark with which they can agree.
[2] "He was a man who had great possessions" is a possible translation; in this case 10:22 belongs by itself.

Passives

13:13 καὶ ἔσεσθε μισούμενοι ὑπὸ πάντων
(There is a possibility that μισούμενοι refers to a future durative state and hence would agree with classical usage. Neither Matthew nor Luke correct.)

All of the above cases of εἶναι with the participle used in place of a regularly conjugated imperfect or future of the verb disagree but slightly with the trend toward such periphrasis observed in the papyri, but the comparatively high number of such cases is a peculiarity of Mark's Greek. We reserve it for examination in part II.

C. Peculiarities in the use of moods

1. The optative in subordinate clauses

Classical Greek employed the optative in relative and temporal sentences to denote frequency or repetition of an occurrence where a single statement would hold for a number of actual occurrences. This single statement as such was not thought of as indicating anything actual: instead of such a statement as "whenever he read a manuscript, he frowned" (repeated occurrence in past time) we have "whenever he would read a manuscript, he would frown"; one abstract statement sufficing for a number of occurrences in past time. This is the so-called iterative optative, but it does not in itself denote repetition (AG I 254,a). An example of this optative is found in the Odyssey:

Γ 217 ὅτε δὴ πολύμητις ἀναΐξειεν Ὀδυσσεύς, στάσκεν

But the indicative also is found (AG I, 254 A.3) and it, like the iterative optative, does not denote actual happenings but serves as a typical statement:

Xen. Anab. 1.8, 1 πᾶσιν οἷς ἐνετύγχανεν ἐβόα

4.7, 16 ᾖδον καὶ ἐχόρευον ὁπότε οἱ πολέμιοι ὄψεσθαι ἔμελλον

In the papyri the iterative optative has almost completely disappeared; the only form persisting is the stereotyped τύχοι (GGP II i 295a), and it is found only in official accounts and statements of grievances:

P. Petr. II 18(2b) 15 ἔτυπτεν αὐτὸν κατὰ τοῦ τραχήλου καὶ ὃ τύχοι μέρος τοῦ σώματος (246a)

P. Magd. 42, 4 πληγάς μοι ἐνέβαλεν καὶ πλείους εἰς ὃ τύχοι μέρος τοῦ σώματος (221a)

In this same papyrus is found the indicative: ὁ ὁπότ' ἠβούλετο and in

PSI V 542, 9 ἔτυπτεν εἰς ὃ ἐτύγχ[ανεν] μέρος τοῦ
σώματος (IIIa)

P. Gurob 8, 12 εἰς ὃ ἔτυχον μέρος τοῦ σώματος (210a)

The iterative optative for designating representative occurrences in past time in relative and temporal sentences has yielded to the indicative in the usage of Mark, and this agrees not only with the trend seen in the papyri, but also with such Hellenistic writings as the history of Polybius (the imperfect appears in iv.32.5; the aorist in iv. 32.6), the LXX (imperfect, Num. 21:9, I Macc. 13:20; aorist, Gen. 30: 42, Ezek. 10:11), the Similitudes of Hermas (imperfect, IX 6, 4; aorist, IX 4, 5 and 17, 3), and the epistle of Barnabas (aorist 12,2). This substitution constitutes an agreement in divergence between Mark and the papyri:

Temporal

3:11 καὶ τὰ πνεύματα...ὅταν αὐτὸν ἐθεώρουν, προσέπιπτον αὐτῷ

11:19 ὅταν (ὅτε AD) ὀψὲ ἐγένετο ἐξεπορεύετο...

Relative

6:56a καὶ ὅπου ἐὰν εἰσπορεύετο...ἐτίθεσαν τοὺς ἀσθενοῦντας

b καὶ ὅσοι ἂν ἥψαντο αὐτοῦ, ἐσώζοντο

## 2. The absence of an apodosis in a conditional sentence (aposiopesis)

Homeric and classical Greek sometimes omit the apodosis to a conditional sentence when omission is rhetorically more effective, e.g.

A (Odyssey) 581 εἴπερ γάρ κ'ἐθέλησιν Ὀλύμπιος ἀστεροπητής ἐξ ἑδέων στυφελίξαι     i.e."if he wishes...what's to stop him?"

Xen. Cyr. VIII 7.24 εἰ μὲν οὖν ἐγὼ ὑμᾶς διδάσκω, οἵους χρὴ πρὸς ἀλλήλους εἶναι- ; εἰ δὲ μή, καὶ παρὰ τῶν προγεγενημένων μανθάνεις;

Similarly, the papyri have examples where the apodosis has been omitted:

P. Hib. 47, 25 καὶ τοὺς μόσχους εἰ μὲν ἀπέσ⟨ταλ⟩κας εἰς Δικωμίαν- · εἰ δὲ μή, ἀπόστειλον ἤδη     (256a)

PSI IV 421, 7 εἰ μὲν διδοῖς ἡμεῖν- · εἰ δὲ μή, ἀποδραμούμεθα     (IIIa)

Mark has one example where a protasis is not followed by an apodosis:

8:12 ἀμὴν λέγω ὑμῖν εἰ δοθήσεται τῇ γενεᾷ ταύτῃ σημεῖον

Aposiopesis, with the exception of the example from Homer, is usually found with a pair of protases:"if..., ...; but if not..., ..." However, there seems to be no ellipse in Mark's failure to state an apodosis; furthermore, the parallels suggest that εἰ is equal to ὅτι.. οὐ. This construction is common in the LXX, e.g. Num. 14:23. We reserve this for consideration among the usages peculiar to Mark.

## 3. Substitute for the imperative

That ἵνα introduced independent clauses as a substitute for the imperative is the testimony of Didymos in scholion to Oedipus Colonus: the line, 156, ἀλλ'ἵνα τῷδ'ἐν ἀφθέγτῳ μὴ προπέσῃς νάπει the scholion, κατὰ τὴν ἡμετέραν συνήθειαν εἰώθαμεν λέγειν οὕτως: ἵνα παραγένῃ πρὸς ἐμε· βούλομαί σοι ⟨τι⟩ σημαίνειν.

The line of Sophocles is said to be the oldest attestation to such a use; and Radermacher (Neutest. Gram. 138) cites from the Acts of Pilate and from Epictetus examples of ἵνα clauses standing independently. The papyri have several examples:

PSI IV 412 1ff (beginning of a ὑπόμνημα Ζήνωνι) ἵνα λαλήσηις Εὐνόμωι περὶ Θήρωνος, ἵνα κομίσηται τὴν τοπαρχίαν καὶ ἐπὶ τῶν αὐτῶν ἦι (IIIa)
(The second ἵνα introduces a substantive clause after λαλήσηις, of course.)

PSI IV 400, 1 περὶ ὧν σοι ἐμπεφάνικα, ἵνα καὶ κομιδήν τινα ποιήσηι πρὸ τοῦ βασιλικὰ γενέσθαι (c.240a)

Negative ἵνα clauses standing independently:

PSI IV 416, 4 (Similarly, at the beginning of a ὑπόμνημα Ζήνωνι) πρὸ τοῦ σε ἀποδημῆσαι ἵνα μέ (= μή) με καταλίπῃς ἐν τῶι δεσμωτηρίωι, οὐ γὰρ ἔχω τὰ ἀναγκαῖα (IIIa)

There is in Mark one example of ἵνα used independently to replace the imperative:

5:23 ἵνα ἐλθὼν ἐπιθῇς τὰς χεῖρας αὐτῇ...

νά with the subjunctive of the second and third persons is used in modern Greek as a substitute for the imperative. It is not without an example in the classical period; it is usual in the Hellenistic period to such an extent that it can be called a divergence with which Mark agrees.

Besides the classical substitute for the imperative of ἵνα with the subjunctive there is another found in the papyri: θέλω with the infinitive as well as with ἵνα and the subjunctive:

BGU III 824, 6 δὲ γινώσκ[ι]ν σε θέλωι, ὅτει κτλ. (55/56p)

844, 3 [Γ]εινώσκειν σε θέλω, ὅτει κτλ. (83p)

In the New Testament are found instances of θέλω with the infinitive and with clauses introduced with ἵνα --in one case occurring in the same verse: I Cor. 14:5 θέλω δὲ πάντας ὑμᾶς λαλεῖν γλώσσαις, μᾶλλον δὲ ἵνα προφητεύητε.

These are found in Mark and constitute an item of agreement in divergence with the papyri:

6:25 θέλω ἵνα ἐξαυτῆς δῶς μοι -         Matt. "δος"

10:35 θέλομεν ἵνα ὃ ἐὰν αἰτήσωμέν σε ποιήσῃς ἡμῖν

### 4. The infinitive

#### a. The infinitive as the complement of certain verbs

##### 1. The infinitive with προλαμβάνω

Jannaris (Histor. Greek Grammar 2121) supposes that προλαμβάνω is used for φθάνω in Mark 14:8: προέλαβεν μυρίσαι μου τὸ σῶμα εἰς τὸν ἐνταφισμόν. The usage occurs in Josephus: Ant. vi.13.7 προύλαβες καταμειλίξασθαί μου τὸν θυμόν. Blass-Debrunner compare II Clem. 8:2 προφθάσῃ βαλεῖν; Jannaris, II Clem.18:23 ἐκβαίνειν ἔφθασας. These prove that the construction is permissible Greek, and the Josephus citation is an independent attestation to the use of προλαμβάνω for φθάνω.

##### 2. Pleonasm of ἄρχομαι with the infinitive

Mark's extensive use of ἄρχομαι with the infinitive where the two are equal to nothing more than the finite form of the verb with which the former appears is without parallel in the papyri but instances of the use of a weak ἄρχομαι are found in Xenophon and Aristophanes. Examples from Xenophon are as follows:

Cyr. i.1.5 ἀνηρτήσατο δὲ τοσαῦτα φῦλα ὅσα καὶ διελθεῖν ἔργον ἐστίν, ὅποι ἄν τις ἄρξηται πορεύεσθαι ἀπὸ τῶν βασιλείων, ἥν τε πρὸς ἕω ἥν τε πρὸς ἑσπέραν ἥν τε πρὸς ἅ.

Anab. vi.1.22 ὅτε ἤρχετο ἐπὶ τὸ συνεπιμελεῖσθαι τῆς στρατίας καθίστασθαι

vii.6.15 ἐπεί γε μὴν ψεύδεσθαι ἤρξατο Σεύθης περὶ τοῦ μισθοῦ, εἰ μὲν ἐπαινῶ αὐτόν, δικαίως ἄν με καὶ αἰτιῶσθε καὶ μισοῦτε

Hellen. iii.4.18 ἐπεὶ δὲ καὶ ἤρξατο προσάγειν τινας τῷ Ἁγησιλάῳ ὁ Λύσανδρος

Mem. iii.5.22 ἀλλ'οἶμαί σε οὐδὲν ἧττον ἔχειν εἰπεῖν ὁπότε στρατηγεῖν ἢ ὁπότε παλαίειν ἤρξω μανθάνειν

With λέγειν-

Anab. iii.1.34 ἤρχετο λέγειν ὧδε·

v.6.28 ἐθυόμην περὶ αὐτοῦ τούτου, εἰ ἄμεινον εἴη ἄρχεσθαι λέγειν εἰς ὑμᾶς καὶ πράττειν

There are in Mark 26 cases where ἄρχομαι is used. Hunkin (JTS xxv p. 391) says that 3 of the 26 instances distinctly mean "begin"; my count is 5. We have but 2 in common.[1] We agree that ἄρχομαι is used in a definitely quasi-auxiliary sense in 6:7, 10:32, and 13:5 (ibid. 392); of the other 18 cases, listed as "doubtful," the use of a finite form in the Matthaean or Lucan parallel in 8 instances indicates that these as well are quasi-auxiliary. That is to say, in the following Matthew or Luke merely confirm our a priori suspicion that the form of ἄρχομαι is, in each case, unnecessary:[2] 5:17, 6:55, 8:11, 10:28, 41, 11:15, 14:65, 69 (B sa bo read εἰπεῖν in verse 69 instead of ἤρξατο πάλιν λέγειν). In the ten instances still remaining this verb is loosely employed, but we cannot appeal to any fact outside of the Markan text itself to indicate that it is pleonastic:[3] 1:45, 2:23, 5:20, 6:2, 34, 8:32, 10:47, 12:1, 15:8, 18. Thus we now have:

---

[1] His three are 10:47, 14:19, 33. I reject 10:47; at best it is doubtful. I include 8:31 since the passion is mentioned for the first time. 4:1 seems almost a distinct "begin," as well as does 14:71.

[2] There is no Lucan parallel to 6:55; there is a paraphrase in 10:41 and 14:65. 8:11 and 11:15 have a form of ἄρχομαι.

[3] 2:23 and 8:32, although Matthew agrees, seem to use ἄρχομαι pleonastically; 10:47, although the Matthaean parallel is a finite form of the verb (and would indicate that the ἤρξατο is superfluous), may mean "began," as Hunkin says. Similarly, 12:1 seems to mean "began"; Matthew rephrases and Luke retains. 6:20 with Matthew avoiding the ἤρξατο can nevertheless mean "begun" since the teaching was interrupted.

1. Cases where ἄρχομαι distinctly equals "begin"  5
2.   "       "      "    more definitely quasi-auxiliary
                          than "begin"  3
3.   "       "      "    has a quasi-auxiliary status con-
                          firmed by parallels  8
4.   "       "           status is doubtful  <u>10</u>
                                              26

We set alongside the figures for Matthew:

1. Distinctly equal "begin"[1]  7
2. Doubtful  5
3. More definitely quasi-auxiliary than "begin"  <u>0</u>
                                                  12

And for Luke:

1. Distinctly "begin"  13
2. Doubtful  14
3. More definitely quasi-auxiliary than "begin"  <u>0</u>
                                                  27

Although parallels from Xenophon have been adduced, the considerations listed immediately above indicate that in pleonastic ἄρχομαι we have a specifically Marcan feature; it will accordingly be further discussed in part II.

### b. Periphrasis of the infinitive- substitution of πῶς for ὡς

The Greek of Mark in common with that of Matthew, Luke, Paul, and Epictetus (Radermacher, op.cit.159) has instances of the interrogative particle πῶς used in place of ὡς and ὅτι which, with a finite verb, introduce clauses used as equivalents of an infinitive clause in indirect discourse where there is no question, direct or indirect, but merely the content of the idea used substantively with a verb of saying, perceiving, or believing. In modern Greek πῶς has completely replaced ὅτι in such a use. The point of departure for such a usage is found in a sentence like the following from the papyri, where πῶς stands for

---

[1]Hunkin finds (ibid. 393) that there are five instances where "begin" is distinctly meant; however, of the doubtful ones two are parallels to Mark 13:31 and 14:71 (Matt. 16:21 and 26:74) which we have already said can be proper uses of ἄρχομαι. Also Matt. 12:1 and 16:32, paralleled by Mark 2:23 and 8:32, may be pleonastic uses.

the Attic ὡς but where also an indirect question may be understood:

BGU 37 οἶδα γὰρ πῶς αὐτοῦ ἑκάστης ὥρας χρῄζωι (51p)

And in Mark πῶς is used after ἀναγινώσκειν and θεωρεῖν:

12:26 οὐκ ἀνέγνωτε...πῶς εἶπεν αὐτῷ ὁ θεός

41 ἐθεώρει πῶς ὁ ὄχλος βάλλει χαλκόν...

c. ἐν with the dative of the articular infinitive

An example of the use of the preposition ἐν with the dative of the articular infinitive for a temporal designation where classical Greek would employ a genitive absolute is not lacking in the papyri:[1]

PSI IV 354 12 ἐν τῷ παραπορεύεσθαι τὸν βασιλέα (254a)

An example showing the transition from the classical use of ἐν τῷ plus the infinitive is the following:

P. Ox. IV 743 35 ἐν τῷ δέ με περισπᾶσθαι οὐκ ἠδυνάσθην συντυχεῖν Ἀπολλω(νίωι) (2a)
(The meaning apparently is both "during" and "due to the fact that")[2]

In Mark the temporal use of ἐν with the articular infinitive does not disagree with the papyri:

4:4 καὶ ἐγένετο ἐν τῷ σπείρειν ὃ μὲν ἔπεσεν κτλ.

6:48 καὶ ἰδὼν αὐτοὺς βασανιζομένους ἐν τῷ ἐλαύνειν

Let us consider these facts: that in 4:4 καὶ ἐγένετο appears with the articular infinitive in a designation of time, that in 1:9 καὶ ἐγένετο appears with a time designation, ἐν ἐκείναις ταῖς ἡμέραις, and that in 6:48 ἐν τῷ with the infinitive is used purely as a time reference. In two cases a time designation follows καὶ ἐγένετο but they are different kinds of designations. In two cases ἐν τῷ is

---

[1] Examples of ἐν τῷ with the infinitive in the sense of "consisting in" are found in Attic but hardly in that of "during."

[2] Moulton cites P.Par. 63, 94 (Gr.N.T.Gr.Proleg.14) τίς οὕτως ἐστιν ἀνάλητος ἐν τῶι λογίζεσθαι καὶ πράγματος διαφορὰν εὑρεῖν (164a) but apparently there is no temporal connotation here.

used with the meaning "during" and one of these appears with καὶ ἐγένετο. The only question we can ask here is: does the use of the dative of the articular infinitive in a sense other than that of the Attic one of "consisting in,' namely, that of "during," have support in the papyri? The answer we have already tried to give.[1]

5. The participle

a. Pleonasm of the participle

The use of a superfluous participle is confined to the gospels and the LXX. In Mark the frequent use of ἐλθών, ἀφείς, and ἀναστάς leads one to suppose them redundant and they are apparently so in the following:[2]

5:23 ἵνα ἐλθὼν ἐπιθῇς τὰς χεῖρας αὐτῇ
7:25 ἀλλὰ εὐθύς..γυνὴ..εἰσελθοῦσα προσέπεσεν πρὸς τ.π.
12:42 καὶ ἐλθοῦσα μία χήρα πτωχὴ ἔβαλεν λεπτὰ δύο
14:45 καὶ ἐλθὼν εὐθὺς προσελθὼν αὐτῷ λέγει·
16:1 ἵνα ἐλθοῦσαι ἀλείψωσιν αὐτόν

ἀφείς-
4:36 καὶ ἀφέντες τὸν ὄχλον παραλαμβάνουσιν αὐτόν
8:13 καὶ ἀφεὶς αὐτοὺς πάλιν ἐμβὰς ἀπῆλθεν εἰς τὸ πέραν
14:50 καὶ ἀφέντες αὐτὸν ἔφυγον πάντες
12:12 καὶ ἀφέντες αὐτὸν ἀπῆλθον [3]

ἀναστάς-
1:35 καὶ πρωΐ ἔννυχα λίαν ἀναστὰς ἐξῆλθεν
2:14 καὶ ἀναστὰς ἠκολούθησεν αὐτῷ
7:24 ἐκεῖθεν δὲ ἀναστὰς ἀπῆλθεν εἰς τὰ ὅρια Τύρου

---

[1] The construction is frequent in the LXX. Radermacher says (op.cit. 151), following Krapp: "The historians of the period from the second century B.C. to the close of the first century A.D. made extensive use of this construction."
[2] The particle in 10:49 is probably not redundant: καὶ στὰς ὁ Ἰησοῦς εἶπεν.
[3] The examples with ἀφείς are not so clearly redundant.

10:1 καὶ ἐκεῖθεν ἀναστὰς ἔρχεται εἰς τὰ ὅρια τῆς Ἰ.

The use of the participle of one verb of saying with a finite form of another verb of saying is, according to Kühner-Gerth (AG II, 585, 6), a part of the classical practice of using the finite form of a verb with the participle of the same verb or one of related meaning, e.g. Soph. Ajax 757 ὡς ἔφη λέγων. In the writings of Herodotus we find a duplication of the verb of saying in participle and finite form:

vi.67.10   εἶπε φάς

68.5   ἔφη...λέγων

The papyri have the following example:

P. Giss. 36, 10 τάδε λέγει Ἀμμωνία καὶ Ἀπολλωνία καὶ Ἡράκλεα καὶ Ἡραὶς αἱ τέτταρες λέγουσαι        (135a)

There are two examples in Mark, in themselves no disagreement with what we find in Sophocles, Herodotus, and the papyrus Giss. 36:

8:28 οἱ δὲ εἶπαν αὐτῷ λέγοντος ὅτι κτλ.

12:26 πῶς εἶπεν αὐτῷ ὁ θεὸς λέγων·

The use of the participle of ἀποκρίνομαι with a finite verb of saying is not found in classical Greek. The papyri have examples with ἀποκρίνεσθαι in the finite form with the participle of a verb of saying:

PSI IV 340, 5   ἀποκέκριται τοιαῦτα λέγων        (257a)

P. Par. 35, 30   ἀπεκρίθησαν φήσαντες        (163a)

In Mark the participle of ἀποκρίνεσθαι with a verbum finitum of saying appears to be pleonastic. In three instances it is 'strictly redundant" because no reply is called for:

9:5 καὶ ἀποκριθεὶς ὁ Πέτρος λέγει τῷ Ἰησοῦ

11:14 καὶ ἀποκριθεὶς εἶπεν αὐτῇ

12:25 καὶ ἀποκριθεὶς ὁ Ἰησοῦς ἔλεγεν

In one case a finite form of ἀποκρίνεσθαι appears asyndetically:

12:29 ἀπεκρίθη ὁ Ἰησοῦς ὅτι κτλ.

In one case there is the same construction as we saw in the papyri:

15:9 ὁ δὲ Πειλᾶτος ἀπεκρίθη αὐτοῖς λέγων

Coördinate with λέγει:

7:28 ἡ δὲ ἀπεκρίθη καὶ λέγει (hist. pres.) αὐτῷ

In the bulk of the examples, however, it appears participially with λέγειν in the form ἀποκριθεὶς λέγει; the extensive use of it in the gospel leads us to reserve this usage for consideration in part II.

b. The genitive absolute

In classical grammar the noun or pronoun in a genitive absolute could not be present in the main clause of the sentence (ibid.II, 78). But exceptions make their appearance as early as Xenophon, Herodotus, and Thucydides; instances where the subjects of the genitives absolute and those of the main clause are the same are:

Thuc. 3.13 βοηθησάντων ὑμῶν προθύμως πόλιν προσλήψεσθε κτλ.

Xen. Cyr. 6.3.17 εἰπόντες δὲ Κύρου... ἔφη (Κῦρος)

Cases where the subject of the genitive absolute appears in the accusative are:

Xen. Cyr.1.5.5 δεξαμένου τοῦ Κύρου οἱ β. ...αἱροῦνται αὐτὸν ἄρχοντα (τὸν Κ.)

Herod. 9.99 οἱ Σάμιοι ἀπικομένων Ἀθηναίων αἰχμαλώτων... τούτους λυσάμενοι πάντας ἀποπέμπουσι ἐς Ἀθήνας

Cases where the noun or pronoun of the genitive absolute is in the dative:

Thuc. 1.114 καὶ ἐς αὐτὴν διαβεβηκότος ἤδη Περικλέους... ἠγγέλθη αὐτῷ (Περικλ.)

Herod. 2.162 λέγοντος αὐτοῦ τῶν τις Αἰγυπτίων ὄπισθε

στὰς περιέθηκε οἱ κυνέην

The development seen in its beginnings in the late classical period finds abundant attestation in the papyri:

Genitive absolute whose subject is identical with a subsequent accusative-

PSI IV 352, 5 βουλομένου ( sc.μοῦ) ποιεῖν σοι πλεῖόν τι αἰσθόμενοι ἐπαρώινησάν με (254a)

BGU VIII 1821, 18 κατακλείσαντές με, ἐμοῦ μηδὲν ἁπλῶς ὀφείλοντος (concluding verb lost) (51-50a)

With a subject identical with that of the main clause-

BGU VIII 1828, 5 γεγεωργηκότος μου ἐν τῶι πρότερον Ἀγελάου κλήρωι προῆγμαι τὴν τοῦ ὑπομνήματος ἐπίδοσιν ποιήσασθαι (52-51a)

BGU II 595, 12 καὶ Ἀμμωνᾶτος καὶ Πασίωνος καταβάντων τὸ αὐτὸ εἴρηχαν κτλ. (70-80p)

With a subject identical with a dative-

P. Lond. III 897, 7 ὠμόσας διὰ τῆς ἐπιστολῆς ὅτι σου παραγενομένου οὐδεμία σοι ἐπήρια ἔσται κτλ. (84p)

BGU IV 1097 ἐμοῦ γὰρ λεγούσης αὐτῷ μὴ στρατεύσῃ, λέγει μοι ὅτι κτλ. (time of Claudius or Nero)

With a subject identical with a subsequent genitive so that the one appears pleonastic-

P. Lille 8, 7 ἀφείρηταί μου Κρησίλαος ζεύγη ταυρικὰ οὐδὲν ὀφείλοντος ἐμοῦ αὐτῶι (IIIa)

P. Hib. 78, 1 πλεονάκις μου γεγραφηκότος σοι οὐδέποτε ὑπακήκοας ἡμῶν (= ἐμοῦ) (244-43a)

Mark is fully within this Hellenistic departure from the classical standard. Examples of identity in subject of a main clause and of a genitive absolute are the following:

6:22 καὶ εἰσελθούσης τῆς θυγατρος αὐτῆς ... καὶ

ὀρχησαμένης ἤρεσεν τῷ Ἡρώδῃ

With a subsequent dative-

5:2 καὶ ἐξελθόντες αὐτοῦ ἐκ τοῦ πλοίου εὐθὺς ὑπήντησεν αὐτῷ κτλ.

9:9 καὶ καταβαινόντων αὐτῶν...διεστείλατο αὐτοῖς

13:1 καὶ ἐκπορευμένου αὐτοῦ...λέγει αὐτῷ

With an accusative-

5:18 καὶ ἐμβαίνοντος αὐτοῦ...παρεκάλει αὐτόν...

21 διαπεράσαντος τοῦ Ἰησοῦ...συνήχθη...ἐπ'αὐτόν

10:17 καὶ ἐκπορευομένου αὐτοῦ...εἰς αὐτὸν ἐπηρώτα

11:27 καὶ ἐν τῷ ἱερῷ περιπατοῦντας αὐτοῦ ἔρχονται πρὸς αὐτόν

13:3 καὶ καθημένου αὐτοῦ εἰς τὸ ὄρος...ἐπηρώτα αὐτόν

With a genitive-

9:28 καὶ εἰσελθόντος αὐτοῦ...οἱ μαθηταὶ αὐτοῦ

10. Particles

A. Negations

1. μή with the participle

Participles expressing statements of fact which can be resolved into declarative sentences, e.g. causal participles, are negated in Attic by οὐ; those in which a participle stands for a subordinate clause which itself would require, in negation, μή, e.g. conditional participles, by μή, viz.

Xen. Cyr. 2.4, 27 οὐκ ἡγεμόνας ἔχων πλανᾷ ἀνὰ τὰ ὄρη

Herod. 7.101 οὐκ ἀξιόμαχοί εἰσι ἐμὲ ἐπιόντα ὑπομεῖναι μὴ ἐόντες ἄρθμιοι      i.e. "unless they are united..."

οὐ with the participle gives way in the usages of the papyri to μή although not to the extent that it does with the infinitive (GGP II ii 556, 560). With the causal participle, for example, the following table shows how μή comes to dispute the place of οὐ (ibid. 562):

| Causal use- | With οὐ | | | With μή | | |
|---|---|---|---|---|---|---|
| | IIIa | II-Ia | Total | IIIa | II-Ia | Total |
| | 5 | 8 | 13 | 0 | 12 | 12 |

An instance of μή with the causal participle:

BGU 1197, 10 οἱ ἱγερεῖς ( sic) μὴ λαμβάνοντες τὰ ὑποκίμενα ( sic) αὐτοῖς εὐτρέχοντες τῷ ἡγεμόνι ἀπεκομίσαντο (13a)

Two causal participles in Mark are negated by μή instead of by οὐ in keeping with the trend of the papyri:

2:4 καὶ μὴ δυνάμενοι προσενέγκαι αὐτῷ...ἀπεστέγασαν κτλ.

8:1 πάλιν πόλλου ὄχλου καὶ μὴ ἐχόντων τί φάγωσιν

2. Superfluous negatives

The use of οὐ with μή in emphatic negations is common in Attic Greek (AG II, sec. 514). In the papyri, however, we find οὐ used with οὐ μή:

Wilcken, Chr. 122, 4 οὐδ'οὐ μὴ γένηται (6p)

The use is found also in Mark 14:25 οὐκέτι οὐ μὴ πίω.

B. Conjunctions

1. ὅτι introductory

There is one example in Mark where ὅτι is ordinarily construed as causal:

8:24 βλέπω τοὺς ἀνθρώπους ὅτι ὡς δένδρα ὁρῶ περιπατοῦντας
"...men, whom I perceive as trees walking about" (?) rather than "for I perceive them"

The D reading βλέπω τοὺς ἀνθρώπους ὡς δένδρα περιπατοῦντας is probably a correction of the above, which is the text of ℵ B. Black (An Aramaic Approach, p. 37) sees the reading of the latter texts as the result of the failure of a translator to recognize an instance of emphatic hyperbaton in Aramaic (" I see men that like trees they are walking") and of his taking the participial present as a true participle and made it to agree with the accusative ἀνθρώπους. The Greek would then require an additional verb ὁρῶ. W.C.Allen (Expository Times, vol. xiii, p. 30, quoted by Black, ibid.) thinks that the Aramaic relative particle d^e was mistranslated by ὅτι, instead of by the relative οὕς. The same kind of an explanation may account for the ὅτι of Mark 6:17 ὅτι ἐγάμησεν αὐτήν.

11. Connection of sentences

A. Asyndeton

The use of such a connecting phrase as ἐν ἐκείναις ταῖς ἡμέραις in Mark (1:9, [2:20 and 4:35 where the singular form is found], 13:17, [19 which has the nominative plural of the expression], 24, [32 which has περὶ τῆς ἡμέρας ἐκείνης], and 14:25 which reads ἕως τῆς ἡμέρας ἐκείνης) has no precedent in Attic nor parallels in the papyri. It is reserved for consideration later.

B. ὅτι recitativum

The use of ὅτι with direct discourse is found in the middle and late classical periods of Attic Greek; the quotations given by Kühner-Gerth (AG II, 367) are, with but two exceptions, from Xenophon and Thucydides. The usage which Mayser terms "volkstümlich" (GGP II iii, 47) abounds in the papyri from the third century B.C. on. An examination of the use of ὅτι recitativum in four letters in Olsson's collection of papyri of the early Roman period (100 B.C.- 100 A.D.) shows that it appears, with possibly one exception,[1] in letters that are not poorly written. In Mark this use is found to a greater extent than in the other gospels (.74 to a page of Tischendorf in Mark; .35 per page in Luke; .13 per page in Matthew). Further, of 23 Matthaean parallels, 21 drop the ὅτι where it is equivalent merely to quotation marks and

---

[1]This exception is a poorly written letter of a freed slave to his patron.

2 retain it; out of 12 Lucan parallels, 8 omit the ὅτι and 4 retain it. Its frequency in Mark seems to be in keeping with the non-literary style of that evangelist.

12. Prepositions

A. Pleonasm of prepositions

The suffix -θεν which, in the classical period, served to answer the question "Whence?" became stereotyped in the Hellenistic period. Examples from the papyri are as follows:

P. Ox. 1216 ἀπὸ μικρόθεν (IIp)

Spec. Isog. pl. xi # 21 (Wilcken, Chr. 176) ἐξ οἰκόθεν

Examples of the--judged by classical standards--superfluous preposition are found in the ἀπὸ μακρόθεν of Mark 5:6, 8:3, 11:13, 14:54, 15:40; in the ἀπὸ ἄνωθεν of 15:38; and in the ἐκ παιδόθεν of 9:21.

Part II Unexplained Markan Usages

1. The use of ἴδε with a nominal sentence (I.1)

The use of ἴδε with a nominal sentence has been set aside for special consideration (page 5). In the LXX ἴδε appears twice as a translation of הנה. The various uses of the word are as follows:

Gen. 27:6 ἴδε εγὼ ἤκουσα τοῦ πατρός σου (translates הנה )

Ju. 19:24 ἴδε (A has ἰδού ) ἡ θυγάτηρ μου ἡ παρθένος καὶ ἡ παλλακὴ αὐτοῦ (translates הנה ; is a nominal sentence)

1 Chr. 21:23 ἴδε δέδωκα τοὺς μόσχους ( translates ראה )

One example of ἴδε translating הנה is a nominal sentence; the other may be an imperative, as is generally the case in the LXX, with the usual relation to the rest of the sentence. ἰδού, on the other hand, is generally an exclamatory particle, and in almost all of the examples is a translation of הנה . In the Aramaic section of Daniel ἰδού (ἴδε does not occur) translates ארו five times, ארו three times and הא once; of these nine instances four are with nominal sentences. Furthermore, this same word appears five times in a section where no Aramaic is at hand to account for the reading of the LXX, that is, where the latter paraphrases; and one of these examples is a nominal sentence. Such an insertion of ἰδού where it does not render any word in the original is found in other parts of the LXX, but the relative frequency of occurrence is highest in Daniel.

ἰδού with a noun in the nominative without a finite verb is quoted by Meisterhans (Gram., sec. 84, 2) from an old Attic inscription ἰδοὺ χελίδων also, Sharp (Epictetus, p. 100) cites Epictetus iv.11. 35 ἰδοὺ νέος ἀξιέραστος ἰδοὺ πρεσβύτης ἄξιος ἐρᾶν καὶ ἀντερᾶσθαι. In the latter citation the use of ἰδού is not that of the interjection but of the imperative, as we find in the papyri:

63

With an accusative-

P. Leid. C recto II 15 ειδου τους χαλκους του αιματος(160a)

With a nominative-

P. Par.51, 25 ἐμὲ δὲ ἄφες, ειδού, πολιὰς ἔχων (159a)

ἴδε retains its imperative force in a papyrus of the first century A.D.:

BGU IV 1079, 28 ἰδέ, ἢ δύναται διὰ Διοδώρου ὑπογραφῆναι ἡ τάβλα διὰ τῆς γυναικὸς τοῦ ἡγεμόνος (41p)

ἰδού however, is an interjection:

P. Ox. 1291 ειδου ἀρτάβηι (=-βη) σοι γίνεται (30p)

BGU 665, II 2 ἰδοὺ ἐπληροφόρησαι αὐτόν (1p)

In Mark's gospel are eight examples of the use of ἴδε, four of which are nominal sentences; and eight examples of the use of ἰδού none of which is a nominal sentence:

2:24 ἴδε τί ποιοῦσιν τοῖς σάββασιν

3:34 ἴδε ἡ μήτηρ μου καὶ οἱ ἀδελφοί μου

11:21 ἴδε ἡ συκῆ ἣν κατηράσω ἐξήρανται

13:1 ἴδε ποταποὶ λίθοι καὶ ποταπαὶ οἰκοδομαί

21 ἴδε ὧδε ὁ Χριστὸς ἴδε ἐκεῖ

15:4 ἴδε πόσα σου κατηγοροῦσιν

35 ἴδε Ἡλείαν φωνεῖ

16:6 ἴδε ὁ τόπος ὅπου ἔθηκαν αὐτόν

1:2 ἰδοὺ ἐγὼ ἀποστέλλω τὸν ἄγγελόν μου

3:32 ἰδοὺ ἡ μήτηρ σου καὶ οἱ ἀδελφοί σου ἔξω ζητοῦσίν σε

4:3 ἰδοὺ ἐξῆλθεν ὁ σπείρων σπεῖραι

10:28 ἰδοὺ ἡμεῖς ἀφήκαμεν πάντα

33 ἰδοὺ ἀναβαίνομεν εἰς Ἱεροσόλυμα

13:23 ἰδοὺ προείρηκα ὑμῖν πάντα

14:41 ἰδοὺ παραδίδοται ὁ υἱὸς τοῦ ἀνθρώπου
42 ἰδοὺ ὁ παραδιδούς με ἤγγικεν

Two verses in the third chapter of this gospel illustrate the difference in the evangelist's use of ἰδού and ἴδε : 3:32 and 34. Remove the ἰδού from any of the examples where it occurs and a complete sentence remains; remove the ἴδε from five of the eight examples and either a verbless nominative or a substantive clause remains. ἴδε, although stereotyped in form like ἄγε, φέρε, tends in Mark's usage to retain its imperative force, even where it has something of the quality of an interjection, e.g. "See! (this is) my mother!" It apparently never becomes a mere interjection like ἰδού in Marcan usage, with the meaning of "lo!" or "behold!"

ἴδε seems to be used in Mark much as ἰδού formerly was.[1] The latter loses its imperative force, as attested by P. Ox. 1291 and BGU 665 and by its constant employment in the LXX to render הנה .[2] ἴδε tends to assume the role of ἰδού in Markan usage--this is to be inferred from its use in the five examples where its removal leaves either a verbless nominative or a substantive clause; in the remaining three examples the force of ἴδε is little more than that of the Marcan ἰδού. If it is conceded that such irregularities as found in the quotations of Meisterhans and Sharp, as well as those of papyri Leiden C and Paris 51, have arisen where no Semitic influence is predicable, Mark's use of ἴδε cannot be viewed as a departure from this.

---

[1] The Latin <u>ecce</u> is used sometimes with an accusative, sometimes with a nominative, and sometimes with a clause, but, like ἰδού loses its imperative force and comes to mean merely "lo!" and "behold!"
[2] It translates ראה 17 times and ראי once.

2. The exaggerated use of the third plural impersonal verb as a substitute for the passive (I.2)

The treatment in part I of the use of the third plural impersonal was closed with the sentence: "As it stands, the practice is not without precedent in the late classical period and parallel in the papyri, but the relatively large number of examples in Mark calls for explanation"(p.8). In the Aramaic section of Daniel a number of impersonal verbs in the third plural are to be found; we shall proceed to observe the way these verbs are rendered by the LXX and by Theodotion:

Dan. 2:13 Aram. ובעו דניאל

LXX ἐζητήθη δὲ ὁ Δανιήλ

Theod. καὶ ἐζήτησαν Δανιήλ

5:3 באדין היתיו מאני דהבא

καὶ ἠνέχθη (τὰ σκεύη)

καὶ ἠνέχθησαν τὰ σκεύη

20 ויקרה העדיו מנה

(vv. 18-22 missing)

καὶ ἡ τιμὴ ἀφῃρέθη ἀπ'αὐτοῦ

23 ולמאניא...היתיו...

καὶ τὰ σκεύη...ἠνέχθη

καὶ τὰ σκεύη...ἤνεγκας (B has ἤνεγκαν–B*, perhaps A also, have –κας)

29a והלבשו לדניאל ארגונא

ὁ βασιλεὺς ἐνέδυσε τὸν Δανιὴλ τὸν πορφύραν κτλ.

καὶ ἐνέδυσαν τὸν Δανιὴλ πορφύραν

29c והכרזו עלוהי

LXX paraphrases

καὶ ἐκήρυξεν (Βαλτασὰρ) περὶ αὐτοῦ...

6:16 (17) והיתיו לדניאל ורמו לגבא

(first part has no equivalent) τότε Δανιὴλ ἐρρίφη εἰς τὸν

λάκκον κτλ.

καὶ ἤγαγον τὸν Δανιὴλ καὶ ἐνέβαλον εἰς τὸν λάκκον

18   -היתית   LXX ἠνέχθη   Theodotion ἤνεγκαν

    -שמה    ἐτέθη          ἐπέθηκαν

(The examples found in the Aramaic in 6:18 are not third plurals: they were included because Theodotion's treatment of them, as compared with the Septuagint's, was instructive.)

24    והיתיו גבריא אלך...רמו

...οἱ δύο ἄνθρωποι ἐκεῖνοι...ἐρρίφησαν τοῖς λέουσι

καὶ ἠγάγοσαν τοὺς ἄνδρας...καὶ εἰς τὸν λάκκον..ἐνεβλήθησαν
           (active to passive)

7:5    וכן אמרין לה

καὶ οὕτως εἶπεν (τὸ θηρίον)

καὶ οὕτως ἔλεγον αὐτῇ

13    וקדמוהי הקרבוהי

καὶ οἱ παρεστηκότες παρῆσαν αὐτῷ

καὶ προσήχθη αὐτῷ

26    ושלטנה יהעדון להשמדה

καὶ τὴν ἐξουσίαν ἀπολοῦσι (καὶ βουλεύσονται) μιᾶναι...

καὶ τὴν ἀρχὴν μεταστήσουσιν τοῦ ἀφανίσαι κτλ.

Results-

Of 12 cases, the LXX changes the active to a passive in       5,
  "     "   has no equivalent in                               1,
  "     "   supplies a subject or changes the construction     4,
  "     "   agrees in the use of a third plural                1,
  "     "   agrees where the Aramaic has a passive             1.

Of 13 cases, Theodotion changes the active to a passive in    3,
             changes the construction in                      2,
             agrees in the use of a third plural              6,
             uses the third plural where Aramaic has a
                        passive                               2.

Observations-

The LXX feels the exaggerated use of the construction is un-Greek and therefore changes it in all but one instance.

Theodotion, extremely literal, sees fit to change it in at least four instances: in one verse (6:24) uses first an active, then a passive, to render two Aramaic third person plural impersonals; and even has a third plural active where the original has a passive singular. Thus, although he usually adheres closely to the Aramaic text, his treatment of the impersonal active used in place of the passive is not consistently literal.

The prominence of words meaning to bring, lead, put and take should be noted; as in Mark, such words form the bulk of the examples.

When we turn to the treatment by the LXX of the Hebrew third plural impersonal we find the following examples (taken at random):

Gen. 29:2   מן הבאר ההיא ישקו העדרים

ἐκ γὰρ τοῦ φρέατος ἐκείνου ἐπότιζον τὰ ποίμνια
(The subject conceivably could be "the children of the east"; however, "shepherds" is probably to be understood. There are three other such impersonals, or verbs with unexpressed subjects, before one comes upon αὐτοῖς in verse 4; apparently a subject for the verbs is thought of as present—that is, one of those here suggested.)

41:14   ויריצהו מן־הבור

καὶ ἐξήγαγεν (Φαραὼ) αὐτὸν ἀπὸ τοῦ ο.

49:31 (occurs three times in all)   שמה קברו את־אברהם

ἐκεῖ ἔθαψαν Ἀβραάμ

1 Sam. 1:25   וישחטו את־הפר ויבאו את־הנער

καὶ ἔσφαξεν (ὁ πατὴρ) τὸν μόσχον καὶ προσήγαγεν Ἄννα κτλ.

23:28   על־כן קראו למקוב ההוא

διὰ τοῦτο ἐπεκλήθη ὁ τόπος ἐκεῖνος..

27:5   יתנו־לי

δότωσαν δή μοι τόπον κτλ.

1 Kg. 1:2   יבקשו לאדני המלך

Ζητησάτωσαν τῷ βασιλεῖ...

15:8   ויקברו אתו בעיר דוד

καὶ θάπτεται... ἐν πόλει Δαυείδ

1 Chr. 11:7   על־כן קראו־לו עיר דויד

διὰ τοῦτο ἐκάλεσεν αὐτὴν Πόλιν Δαυείδ

14:11    על־כן קראו שם־המקום

διὰ τοῦτο ἐκάλεσεν τὸ ὄνομα τοῦ τόπου...

Job 6:2    (והותי Q ) והיתי במאזנים ישאו יחד

(εἰ γάρ τις ἱστῶν) τὰς δὲ ὀδύνας μου ἆραι ἐν ζυγῷ...

Jer. 16:6    ולא־יספדו להם

οὐ μὴ κόψονται αὐτούς κτλ.

Hos. 12:9    כל־יגיעי לא ימצאו־לי

(LXX, 8) πάντες οἱ πόνοι αὐτοῦ οὐχ εὑρεθήσονται αὐτῷ...

Results-

Of 11 (or 18, if the additional impersonals of Gen. 29 and 49 are
                              counted)
examples,   3   record a change to a passive,
            5   supply a subject,
           _3_  follow the Hebrew (counting Gen. 29 and 49, 10),
           11 (18)

Conclusions-

It is not necessarily to be inferred that all cases where the LXX does not follow the Hebrew and render literally an active third person plural imply disapproval; the frequency of such cases, however, strongly suggests such disapproval. The treatment, then, is not greatly different from that of the LXX of the same use in the Aramaic section of Daniel. Of the five cases where a subject is supplied, one (1 Sam. 1:25), may not represent an attempt to get around the difficulty of an impersonal subject. However, the acquiescence in three instances (1 Sam. 27:5, 1 Kg. 1:2, Jer. 16:6) (or ten, if Gen. 29 and 49 are counted) of the Greek with the Hebrew form does not agree with the change which the LXX of Daniel makes in identical circumstances. These three stand as examples of the failure of the translators to view--at least in isolated cases--such a construction as a violation of koine usage.

In the case of Daniel 2:4-7:28, repetition of the usage was apparently felt to be beyond the limits where Hellenistic Greek might go; this seems to be a proper inference from the fact that the Greek follows the Aramaic in using the third plural but once, and has some other construction in nine cases out of twelve. The rest of the OT displays a similar unwillingness to employ the form as a substitute for the passive, although the numerical ratio of seeming disapproval to approval is not large. In the case of a translation as reputedly literal as Theodotion's a large number of third person plurals used in place of a passive is due to the use of such a plural in the original, but the construction is not duplicated in the Greek in every instance.

These conclusions may be stated:

1. Koine Greek apparently disapproves of the frequent use of the third person plural as a substitute for the passive; literal translation Greek, to a much less degree.

2. The frequent use of the third plural indefinite instead of the passive may be attributed, in the case of translation, to such a use in the original.

3. Where translation is questionable (as in Mark) the overworking of the usage may be due to the laxity found in a non-literary style.

### 3. The distributive singular (I.3.C)

The distributive singular has been classed as a phenomenon limited to biblical writings (p. 10); accordingly we will examine the reason for, and tabulate the frequency of, its occurrence in the LXX. We shall first take examples at random:

Gen. 19:10     וישלחו האנשים את־ידם

ἐκτείναντες δὲ οἱ ἄνδρες τας χεῖρας κτλ.

42:28     ויצא לבם

καὶ ἐξέστη ἡ καρδία αὐτῶν

Ex. 14:5     לבב פרעה ועבדיו

   ἡ καρδία Φαραὼ καὶ ἡ καρδία τῶν θεραπόντων...

  8  את־לב פרעה

   ...τὴν καρδίαν Φαραὼ...καὶ τῶν θεραπόντων...

Lev. 26:36  בלבבם

   ...εἰς τὴν καρδίαν αὐτῶν

  41  לבבם

   ...ἡ καρδία αὐτῶν...

Jos. 7:6  על־ראשם...

   ...ἐπὶ τὰς κεφαλὰς αὐτῶν (τὴν κεφαλήν- AF)

Ju. 7:16  ביד־כלם...

   ...ἐν χειρὶ πάντων...

  19  ..בידם...

   ...ἐν ταῖς χερσὶν αὐτῶν...

  25  וראש־ערב וזאב...

   ...καὶ τὴν κεφαλὴν Ὠρὴβ καὶ Ζήβ...

  8:28  וראשם..

   ...κεφαλὴν αὐτῶν...

2 Kg. 11:12  ויכו־כף

   ...καὶ ἐκρότησαν τῇ χειρί...

Ps. 78:36  בפיהם ובלשונם...

   ...ἐν τῷ στόματι αὐτῶν καὶ τῇ γλώσσῃ αὐτῶν...

  144:8  אשר פיהם...

   ...ὧν το στόμα...

Is. 5:25  ...נבלתם...

   ...τὰ θνησιμαῖα αὐτῶν...

Jer. 18:16  כל עובר...בראשו...

   ... πάντες οἱ διαπορευόμενοι...τὴν κεφαλὴν αὐτῶν
             (AQ τὰς κεφαλάς)

Dan. 3:27  בגשמהון...ושער ראשהון

   ...τοῦ σώματος αὐτῶν καὶ αἱ τρίχες αὐτῶν...

Results-

These may be tabulated as follows:

|  | "heart" | "head" | "body" | "mouth" | "hand" | "corpse" | "tongue" | |
|---|---|---|---|---|---|---|---|---|
| Heb. sing. | 5 | 5 | 1 | 2 | 4 | 1 | 1 | 19 |
| plur. | | | | | | | | 0 |
| Gr. sing. | 5 | 4 | 1 | 2 | 2 | | 1 | 15 |
| plur. | | 1 | | | 2 | 1 | | 4 |

Observations-

1. The Hebrew usage is unvarying throughout.

2. Translation Greek follows the Hebrew in the majority of cases.

We have chosen for further examination all the occurrences of the word "heart" in the LXX. Five examples with the singular have been cited; the following have the plural:

1 Sam. 6:6; 7:3; 10:26; 1 Chr. 22:19; 29:18; Job 12:24; Ps. 4:5; 22:26; 27 (28):3; 32 (33):15; 34 (35):25; 47 (48):13; 61 (62):8; 77 (78):18; 80 (81):12 (13); 94 (95):8; Pr. 15:7, 11; Hos. 7:14; 10:2; 13:6; Joel 2:13; Na. 2:7 (8); Zeph. 1:12; Hag. 1:5, 7; 2:16 (15), 19 (18) (bis); Za. 7:10; 8:17; 12:5; Is. 63:17; Lam. 3:41; 5:15; Ez. 14:3, 5; Dan. 11:27 (Theod.).

Results-

Of approximately 134 cases of the distributive singular in the Hebrew, 38, or about 28%, have a plural in the Greek. In general, the equivalent in translation of the word "heart" follows the original but cannot be depended on to indicate in every case the form of that original.

The list of examples on page 10 contains, in addition to those of the LXX and Mark, Luke 1:66, Eph. 6:14, and Rev. 6:11. Of these three instances of the distributive singular, we can be sure that the one in Ephesians is not due to translation (the vocabulary recalls that of Isa. 59:17 and 11:5 where the subject of the equipping is singular; however, the phrase is not imported intact into the locution in Ephesians). Mark has other examples of the distributive idea expressed by a plural:

2:6 καὶ διαλογιζόμενοι ἐν ταῖς καρδίαις αὐτῶν

8 ...ἐν ταῖς καρδίαις ὑμῶν

15:29 κινοῦντες τὰς κεφαλὰς αὐτῶν

Passages where singulars are found are as follows:

3:5 συνλυπόμενος ἐπὶ τῇ πωρώσει τῆς καρδίας αὐτῶν

6:52 ἀλλ'ἦν αὐτῶν ἡ καρδία πεπωρωμένη

7:21 ἔσωθεν γὰρ ἐκ τῆς καρδίας τῶν ἀνθρώπων...

8:17 πεπωρωμένην ἔχετε τὴν καρδίαν ὑμῶν...

If any distinction in Mark's use of the singular and the plural is to be drawn, it is the following: When he employs the distributive in a concrete way he uses the plural;[1] the singular, when a figurative or collective idea is to the fore, e.g. "hardness of heart" (3:5, 6:52, 8:17) or "heart" collectively, as the source of evil (7:28). If this distinction can be maintained, Mark's use of the distributive singular would not seem to require further explanation; if it cannot, the influence of the vocabulary of the LXX--as is probably the case in Eph. 6:14--can be advanced as a reason. The presence of a distributive singular in the LXX, we have already seen, is due to literal rendering but literalness is sometimes abandoned, thus leaving us with a possible control (whereby to test Mark's usage) considerably less than completely reliable.

4. The use of plurals (I.3.D)

The only plural used by Mark which cannot be accounted for by consulting the usage of Attic Greek was that of οὐρανός (page 12). One variety of the Hebrew plural of local extension (G-K, 124, 1) is the "surface plural," in which "the idea of a whole composed of innumerable

---

[1]Viz. 2:6, 8 ἐν ταῖς καρδίαις αὐτῶν ; 15:29 κινοῦντες τὰς κεφαλὰς αὐτῶν...

separate parts or points is...evident" (ibid.124b). Most common of this type of plural is the word שמים. In the LXX there are approximately 450 cases of translation of שמים: with the exception of 36, 27 of which are in the Psalms, all have, not the plural, but the singular. This count includes the instances in the Aramaic portion of Daniel where שמיא is invariably rendered by both Theodotion and the LXX with a singular of the equivalent Greek word. The plural does not occur often enough in the parts of the LXX other than the Psalms to lead us to regard this as a possible biblicism of Mark's. However, the proportion of plural to singular in the Psalms is 1:3 and in Mark, 1:2; and this suggests that a greater familiarity on the part of the evangelist with the Psalms than with the rest of the LXX may have contrbuted to his use of the plural.

5. The use of the nominative in time designations (I.4.A.1)

The variety of readings for Mark 8:2 (-αις τρισίνB 892; -ας τρεῖς 1-118-209, 13-69-346) evinces a common effort to get around the difficulty of the nominative used to denote extent of time.

The solitary example of the nominative used as a time designation in the LXX is Eccles. 2:16:

בשכבר הימים הבאים הכל נשכח

καθότι ἤδη αἱ ἡμέραι ἐρχόμεναι τὰ πάντα ἐπελήσθη

The version is extremely literal as a glance at the next verse (2:17), which translates את־החיים by σὺν τὴν ζώην will show.[1] The translator renders the undifferentiated Hebrew form as a nominative. Another of the three extra-Markan occurrences of this construction is Aquila's rendering of Josh. 1:11:

Heb.     כי בעוד שלשת ימים אתם עברים

---

[1]Barton regards the version now found in the LXX as the work of Aquila (ICC Eccles. 8f).

Aqu. ἔτι τρεῖς ἡμέραι ὑμεῖς διαβήσεσθε

LXX ἔτι τρεῖς ἡμέραι καὶ ὑμεῖς διαβαίνετε

It is instructive to observe the way this Hebrew construction--almost identical in phrasing in most of the cases--is treated in other parts of the LXX:

Gen. 40:13 ἔτι τρεῖς ἡμέραι καὶ μνησθήσεται Φαραὼ τῆς ἀρχῆς σου (nominal sentence with copula omitted)

19 ἔτι τρίων ἡμέρων [D inserts καὶ] ἀφελεῖ Φαραὼ τὴν κεφαλήν σου
(genitive of time within which something occurs; see AG I 386)

Isa. 7:8 ἀλλ'ἔτι ἐξήκοντα καὶ πέντε ἐτῶν ἐκλείψει ἡ β.
(genitive of time within which)

21:16 ὅτι ἐνιαυτὸς ὡς ἐνιαυτὸς μισθωτοῦ, ἐκλείψει ἡ δόξα τῶν υἱῶν Κηδάρ (may be a nominal clause, with the omission of a καί to be attributed to the fact that a series of visions is here given poetical presentation. א inserts a καί between μισθωτοῦ and ἐκλείψει.)

Jer. 28:3 ἔτι δύο ἔτη ἡμέρων καὶ ἐγὼ ἀποστρέψω
(Probably a nominal sentence- although may be acc. of extent.)

Amos 4:7 καὶ ἐγὼ ἀνέσχον ἐξ ὑμῶν τὸν ὑετὸν πρὸ τρίων μηνῶν τοῦ τ.

Examination of the passages just cited shows that, by way of explaining the use of the nominative under consideration, a nominal construction with the καί omitted could conceivably have arisen and that ἤδη might have been substituted for ἔτι (v.supra, p. 13). With but one possible exception, Isa. 21:16, the translators have chosen to give an idiomatic Greek rendering. Aquila gives literal rendering and uses a nominative for the Hebrew designation of time, where we should expect an accusative.

Chapter 8 of Tischendorf's text of the Acts of Paul and Thecla (where the one remaining extra-Markan instance is found) reads in part: καὶ γὰρ ἡμέρας τρεῖς καὶ νύκτας τρεῖς Θέκλα ἀπὸ τῆς θυρίδος οὐκ ἐγείρεται. And P. Ox. I 6, 3 (a fragment of this chapter) has: ἡμέραι γὰρ ἤδη τρεῖς καὶ νύκτες τρεῖς Θέκλα ἀπὸ ταύτης τῆς θυρίδος οὐκ ἐγήγερται. This papyrus is itself of the fifth century A.D. and antedates the text found in Tischendorf by about five centuries.

There is practically no warrant for regarding the use of the nominative in a time designation as conscious or unconscious imitation of the language of the LXX (in the Acts of Paul and Thecla it may be in imitation of Mark's and Matthew's[1] use). Viteau (Sujet, p.41) contends that in Eccles. 2:16 it is a Hebraism and that the LXX has inserted a καί in its translation of Josh. 1:11 to change what would otherwise be a Hebraism into an acceptable Greek construction. In Mark it can hardly be a Hebraism--to account for its presence we must posit either literal translation--since such translation is the explanation for two of three extra-Markan instances of the usage--or a nominal construction from which the καί has been omitted, although concern for good Greek has been responsible for the inserting of a καί in all but one of the examples from the LXX.[2] Thus the balance of probability would rest with literal translation as the reason for the use of the nominative as a time designation in Mark.

6. The nominative with the article in place of the vocative (I.4.B)

Concerning the use of the nominative with the article as a substitute for the vocative Moulton says (i, 70): "...classical Greek shows the idiom well established." Mayser's Grammatik, as we noted above (p. 14), has only examples of the nominative without the article used for the vocative. The only classical examples available are from Aristo-

---

[1] We have used the adjective "extra-Markan" loosely; there is an example of the construction in the Matthaean parallel to Mark 8:2.
[2] But see Allen, (Mark, ad loc.), who cites Lucian, Dial. Mer. α 1 οὐ γὰρ ἑώρακα, πολὺς ἤδη χρόνος, αὐτὸν παρ' ὑμῖν. This would support the ἤδη (εἰσιν) τρεῖς ἡμέραι explanation.

phanes:

    Acharn. 242 προῖθ'εἰς τὸ πρόσθεν ὀλίγον ἡ κανηφόρος
              i.e. "you (who are) the basket-bearer..."

    Ran. 521 ὁ παῖς ἀκολούθει   "you there, the lad I mean..."

    Av. 665 ἡ Πρόκνη, ἔκβαινε

Blass supposes that the circumstances of the address first required the insertion of the article, and that this could only be followed by the nominative (GNTGE 86).

In the LXX are found numerous examples of the nominative of θεός, for example, used with the article in place of the vocative. Further inquiry in the book of Psalms establishes the fact that no article is affixed to the vocative in Hebrew which ὁ θεός translates. Other data:

ὁ θεός translates אלהים 51 times; אל 3 times.

ὁ θεός (sometimes with μοῦ or ἡμῶν) is found, alongside the normal Greek vocative κύριε 14 times, rendering אל , חי-אלהם, אדני יהוה. Once ὁ θεός μου translates צורי. ὁ θεός translates אלהי 8 times. θέε is found but 7 times in the LXX: Ju. 21:3 (A ὁ θεός ); Isa. 38:19 (AS κύριε ); Ezek. 4:14; Sir. 23:4; Wisd. of Sol. 9:1; III Macc. 6:2 and IV Macc. 6:27.

ὁ θεός seems to be a fixed phrase and is used (rather than θεός ) to translate a Hebrew vocative occurring without an article. Other Greek equivalents for Hebrew vocatives are as follows:

    Judg. 3:19 βασιλεῦ- המלך    I Kingd. 17:58(A) παιδάριον-הנער

    I Kingd. 24:9 κύριε βασιλεῦ- אדני המלך

    II Kingd. 14:4 βασιλεῦ- המלך

    III Kingd. 18:26 ὁ Βάαλ- הבעל

    IV Kingd. 9:5 ὁ ἄρχων- השר

An examination of the vocative of βασιλεῦς in the four books of Kingdoms yields no example of the nominative with the article used for the vocative although the Hebrew vocative in every instance has the article. The phrase ὁ θεός μου καὶ ὁ βασιλεῦς μου appears three times in the Psalms, twice rendering אלהי ומלכי and once אלהי המלך. κύριε is the only form used as a vocative of κύριος in the Psalms; similarly, υἱέ and πάτερ in Genesis and the Psalms. πάτερ renders אבי in Gen. 22:7, 27:38 (bis), 48:18; πάτερ μου occurs once for אבי in Gen. 27:18.

The examples of the use of a nominative with the article in place of a vocative are due in the Greek to something else than close adherence to the Hebrew text. In the New Testament, exclusive of the gospels, Acts and Revelation, the nominative with the article replacing the vocative is found in Heb. 1:8 (a quotation from the LXX of Ps. 45:7 where the ὁ θεός stands opposite אלהים ), 10:7 ἰδοὺ ἥκω...τοῦ ποιῆσαι, ὁ θεὸς τὸ θέλημά σου; in Col. 3:16 αἱ γυναῖκες ὑποτάσσεσθε and in Eph. 6:1 τὰ τέκνα.

The foregoing discussion shows that a nominative used with the article in place of the vocative is not necessarily due to translation. It suggests that certain fixed equivalents for the vocative were used in the Greek with no reference to the precise form of the original. However, we cannot decide whether the τὸ ἄλαλον καὶ κῶφον πνεῦμα has the article because it translates a Semitic vocative (the translation phenomena from the LXX are against this) or because it is a possible koine usage (as ὁ θεός and αἱ γυναῖκες can be said to be; and it may be questioned whether αἱ γυναῖκες and τὰ τέκνα are real vocatives but rather are not more definite indications of the persons addressed). It is to be noted that the evangelist does not say he is translating, as he does in 5:41 and 15:34 (cf. θύγατερ in 5:34), but even where he says as much the article may not be due to literal adherence to an original.

7. The dative with πιστεύειν ἐν (I.4.E.1)

Moulton, having at first asserted that the use of ἐν with πιστεύω "was suggested no doubt by its being a more literal translation of the Hebrew phrase with בְּ but in itself...was entirely on the line of development of the Greek language" (op.cit. Proleg. 67), afterward under the influence of Burkitt, who compared Jer. 12:6: μὴ πιστεύσῃς ἐν αὐτοῖς ὅτι λαλοῦσιν πρὸς σὲ καλά , accepted the usage as translation Greek.[1] Besides the passage from Jeremiah there are two others in the LXX where ἐν with πιστεύω occurs:

Ps. 77:22 ὅτι οὐκ ἐπίστευσαν ἐν τῷ θεῷ

כי לא האמינו באלהים

Dan. 6:23 (Θ) ὅτι ἐπίστευσαν ἐν τῷ θεῷ αὐτοῦ (A omits ἐν)

(24) די הימן באלהה

πιστεύειν in the majority of cases in the LXX is rendered without an ἐν, due to the avoiding of a construction outside the Greek Sprachgefühl; its presence in Theodotion, coupled with the impossibility of its meaning in any of those instances "within the sphere of..." (as Deissmann maintained for Mark 1:15- In Christo Jesu, 46) makes it very likely that the locution from Mark 1:15 is also translation Greek (that of either the LXX or of some other Greek translation of the OT).

8. The use of the phrase διὰ χειρός as a periphrasis for αὐτῷ (I.5.B.1.a)

διὰ χειρός with the genitive is conceded by Howard to be "based on the Hebrew and Aramaic phrase ביד but it is not a literal translation" (op.cit. II 462). The phrase διὰ χειρός occurs in the papyri,

---

[1] I append a note of Howard's: "FCB to JHM (letter 30/8/10): οὐκ ἐπιστεύσατε αὐτῷ (Mark 11:31= Matt. 21:25) is translated by the Old Syriac, 'believed not in him;' in the Peshitta it is 'believed not him.' The Peshitta is literal; the Old Syriac gives the Aramaic idiom."

meaning "from hand to hand":

P. Magd. 25, 2 ὀφείλων γὰρ μ[ο]ι διὰ χερὸς κριθῶν(ἀρτάβας) τε (221a)

P. Fay. 92, 18 δραχμὰς πεντήκοντα ἐξ παραχρῆμα διὰ
χιρὸς (sic) ἐξ οἴκου (126p)

P. Ox. 268, 7 ἀπεσχηκυῖαι [παρὰ τοῦ Ἀντ]ιφάνους διὰ
χειρὸς[ἐ]ξ οἴκου ὃ καὶ ἐπε[ἰσθη]σαν κεφάλαιον (58p)

An examination of the reasons why the expression occurs in the LXX will show that it is not altogether a literal translation:

It translates      ביד      15 times
                    על־יד      3 times
                    מיד      1 time

The phrase usually renders ביד but in the majority of cases ביד is translated ἐν χειρί. διὰ χειρός occurs 5 times in Genesis, 14 times in I and II Chronicles, and 3 times in Ezekiel; there is one occurrence in each of the following: Leviticus, Joshua, III Kingdoms, and Judith. Besides these examples, the phrase is found in the Wisdom of Solomon, which is not a translation--at least in this portion[1]--but written by one "whose memory is stored with expressions drawn from the book of his daily meditation (i.e., the LXX)" (Gregg, Cam. Bible xv); and in I Maccabees, which, it is generally conceded, is a translation of a Semitic original.

Observations-

1. The examples of διὰ χειρός found in the papyri are not coupled to a genetival noun or pronoun; those in Mark and the LXX are.

2. The idea that a person or persons is the direct agent is not to the fore in the examples from the papyri as it is in those from Mark

---

[1] Purinton (JBL xlvii 304) argues for a Hebrew original for a part of the Wisdom of Solomon; his concluding sentence is:"Such considerations lead one to believe that the original Wisdom of Solomon written in Hebrew extended as far as 11:1 of the present Greek text." Ours is 12:1.

and the LXX.

3. The words are not a literal rendering of any Semitic phrase; and the Greek locution is the same throughout the examples from the LXX; the Hebrew is the same in the majority of instances (15 out of 19).

4. One example (Wisdom of Solomon) is to be attributed to thought environment rather than to translation.

5. Nearly all the instances of διὰ χειρός occur in three books, Genesis, Chronicles (I & II), and Ezekiel, whereas a glance at a Hebrew concordance shows that the usage of ביד with a suffix or noun is uniformly distributed throughout the whole of the Masoretic text.

Conclusions-

(1) and (2) taken together rob of some of its plausibility the contention that the locution is "obviously modelled upon the vernacular phrase διὰ χειρός of money paid 'by hand', 'directly'" (Moulton and Milligan, Vocab. NT p. 145); that the phrase in the Greek lay ready as a vehicle for the Semitic thought must not be disallowed, however. (3), (4), and (5) further support the inference that the locution is Semitic in essence only. Although ἐν χειρί is much more frequent in the LXX than διὰ χειρός the latter is probably to be classified among Markan usages as a biblicism (the expression also occurs in Acts 19:11,26; in the former it equals Παύλῳ). The possibility of a Semitism of thought employing a current Greek phrase (and as such belonging to the koine) may be noted.

9. The use of ἐπί with the accusative as a substitute for περί with the genitive (I.5.C.1.b)

The use of ἐπί and the accusative with σπλαγχνίζεσθαι and with γράφειν where περί and the genitive would be proper has been designated a Markism (page 31). The LXX has no examples of σπλαγχνίζεσθαι ἐπί with the accusative; we are reminded of רחם על the one instance of which in the Old Testament is translated as follows:

81

Ps. 103:13 καὶ καθὼς οἰκτείρει πατὴρ υἱοὺς οἰκτείρησεν Κύριος τοὺς φοβουμένους αὐτόν

על with the noun רחמים appears twice:

I Kg. 3:26 נכמרו רחמיה על־בנה

ὅτι ἐταράχθη ἡ μήτρα αὐτῆς ἐπὶ τῷ υἱῷ αὐτῆς

Ps. 114:9 רחמיו על־כל־מעשיו

καὶ οἱ οἰκτειρμοὶ αὐτοῦ ἐπὶ πάντα τὰ ἔργα αὐτοῦ ("over")

An allusion to Isa. 27:11 is made in the Tractate B'rakhoth:

33a כל מי...אסור לרחם עליו
"It is forbidden to have mercy upon one who does not possess knowledge..."

and Sabb. 151 b (referring to Dt. 13:18):

כל המרחם...מרחמים עליו
"...he who shows...mercy to men will be shown...mercy in heaven."

All the other examples of the verb רחם meaning "to have compassion upon" take a direct object.

The books of Joshua, Job, and Hosea, examined, yielded no instance of ἐπί and the accusative translating על in the sense of "concerning." There is the following example of ἐπί and the accusative where the ἐπί is plainly a literal equivalent of על:

Job 31:1 ומה אתבונן על־בתולה

καὶ οὐ συνήσω ἐπὶ παρθένον

"Concerning" is hardly to be read here; rather is it "look upon" with the ἐπί rendering the "upon." Lack of correspondence between the Hebrew and the Greek robs any inference here of decisive value; there is, however, an equivalence between על־בתולה and ἐπὶ παρθένον.

Greek equivalents for על where it is used in the sense of "concerning" follow:

περί-

Gen. 26:21 ἐκρίνοντο δὲ καὶ περὶ ἐκείνου...

41:15 ἐγὼ δὲ ἀκήκοα περὶ σοῦ κτλ.

Ju. 9:3 καὶ ἐλάλησον περὶ αὐτοῦ οἱ ἀδελφοί
II Kg. 14:8 κἀγὼ ἐντελοῦμαι περὶ σοῦ
III Kg. 10:6 ὁ λόγος ὃν ἤκουσα...περὶ τοῦ λόγου κτλ.
22:8 ὅτι οὐ λαλεῖ περὶ ἐμοῦ καλά κτλ.
IV Kg. 6:11 καὶ ἐξεκινήθη ἡ ψυχὴ...περὶ τοῦ λόγου τούτου
8:5 βοῶσα πρὸς τὸν βασιλέα περὶ τοῦ οἴκου ἑαυτῆς
II Esd. (Neh.) 11(1):6 ἣν ἐγὼ προσεύχομαι...περὶ υἱῶν
Ἰσραήλ κτλ.
Isa. 2:1 ὁ λόγος ὁ γενόμενος πρὸς Ἡσαΐαν υἱὸν Ἀμὼς περὶ
τῆς Ἰ.
Jer. 16:3 ὅτι τάδε λέγει Κύριος περὶ τῶν υἱῶν καὶ περὶ
τῶν θ.
33:4 ὅτι οὕτως εἶπεν Κύριος περὶ οἴκων κτλ.

ὑπέρ-

III Kg. 5:13 καὶ ἐλάλησεν ὑπὲρ τῶν ξύλων κτλ.
11:10 καὶ ἐντειλαμένῳ αὐτῷ ὑπὲρ τοῦ λόγου τούτου
Joel 1:3 ὑπὲρ αὐτῶν τοῖς τέκνοις ὑμῶν διηγήσασθε

κατά-

I Kg. 27:11 Μὴ ἀναγγείλωσιν εἰς Γὲθ καθ'ἡμῶν
Ps. 27:5 Ἐξαγορεύσω κατ'ἐμοῦ τὴν ἁμαρτίαν κτλ.
Isa. 1:1 ὅρασις...ἣν εἶδεν κατὰ τῆς Ἰουδαίας

The Greek translations of the Aramaic section of the book of Daniel were canvassed for equivalents for the Aramaic preposition על where the meaning is "concerning":

2:15 LXX ...περὶ τίνος...

Theodotion ...περὶ τίνος

18 περὶ τοῦ μυστηρίου τούτου
ὑπὲρ τοῦ μυστηρίου τούτου

5:14 (no parallel)    16 (paraphrased)
ἤκουσα περὶ σοῦ        περὶ σοῦ

29    (no parallel)
         ...περὶ αὐτοῦ...
6:18 (19) ...περὶ τοῦ Δανιήλ...
         (no parallel)
7:16   ὑπὲρ πάντων τούτων
       περὶ πάντων τούτων
19     περὶ τοῦ θηρίου
         ditto
20     περὶ τῶν δέκα κεράτων αὐτοῦ
         ditto

In this section there are two instances where the LXX renders על by ἐπί; Theodotion, however, has περί in both cases:

3:16   ἐπὶ τῇ ἐπιταγῇ ἀποκριθῆναί σοι
       περὶ τοῦ ῥήματος τούτου
6:14 (15) ἐλυπήθη ἐπὶ τῷ Δανιήλ
       καὶ περὶ τοῦ Δανιὴλ ἠγωνίσατο

The following are the cases where ἐπί and the accusative render an Aramaic על (whatever the sense):

2:49  LXX κατέστησεν ἐπὶ τῶν πραγμάτων     "over"
       Theodotion  "  ἐπὶ τὰ ἔργα
3:12   κατέστησας ἐπὶ τῶν ἔργων            "over"
         "       ἐπὶ τὰ ἔργα
19     καὶ ἡ μορφή...ἠλλοιώθη ἐπὶ Σεδράχ (case?) "against?"
         ditto
4:13 (Theod. only) καὶ ἑπτὰ καιροὶ ἀλλαγήσονται ἐπ' αὐτόν "over"
14 (Theod. only) καὶ οὐδέν ἦμα ἀνθρώπων ἀναστήσει ἐπ' αὐτήν, "over"
20 (Theod. only) ἑπτὰ καιροὶ ἀλλοιωθῶσιν ἐπ' αὐτόν "over"
22 (Theod. only) καὶ ἑπτὰ καιροὶ ἀλλαγήσονται ἐπὶ σέ "over"
25 (Theod. only) ταῦτα πάντα ἔφθασεν ἐπὶ Ν. τὸν βασιλέα
29 (Theod. only) (the same as verse 22)

30 ὁ λόγος συνετελέσθη ἐπὶ N. (LXX ἐπὶ σέ)"against"
   or "upon"
31 (Theod. only) καὶ αἱ φρένες μου ἐπ'ἐμὲ ἐπεστράφησαν
   "to"
33 (Theod. only) (the same as verse 31)

Observations:

1. The locution "have mercy upon" is biblical Hebrew and an equivalent in idiomatic Greek is at hand for the one instance in the Masoretic text. There are phrases with ἐπί (once with the dative and once with the accusative) which render the parallel use of the noun רחמים with על. It cannot be a biblicism.[1]

2. ἐπί and the accusative, on the basis of an examination of its use in three books selected at random, Joshua, Hosea, and Job, is not used to translate על where it means "concerning."

3. The Hebrew preposition על meaning "concerning" is rendered in the LXX by περί, ὑπέρ or κατά -- the last-named being used because a statement is not only about, but adverse to, a subject.[2]

4. The Aramaic preposition על where it means "concerning," is generally translated by περί with the genitive (there are two examples with ὑπέρ and the genitive); the LXX has ἐπί with the dative twice.[3]

5. ἐπί with the accusative in rendering the Aramaic is generally to be translated "against" or "over"--both of which translations Attic Greek allowed.

These observations make no conclusions possible as to the equivalence of על and ἐπί where the latter means in translation "con-

---

[1]The verb σπλαγχνίζεσθαι first appears in biblical Greek; Lightfoot thinks it (Philip. 1:8) "perhaps a coinage of the Jewish dispersion." Delitzsch renders the passage Mk. 1:41 וירחם עליו (quoted by Swete, Mark, ad loc.).
[2]III Kg. 21:4 (A) καὶ ἐκλελυμένος ἐπὶ τῷ λόγῳ translating the Hebrew על , is not a real exception to this statement: the meaning is not "concerning" (so BDB 754g) because there is no end-object signification here-- only a cause object; only an end-object meaning is allowed for the word "concerning."
[3]The dative with ἐπί denoting the reason for an action is permissible Greek.

cerning." We turn to the treatment of the Hebrew preposition אל in the LXX where it appears with verbs of telling, saying, narrating etc. in the sense of "concerning":

Gen. 20:2 εἶπεν δὲ Ἀβραὰμ περὶ Σάρρας κτλ.

43:30 (Heb.)

(LXX translates רחמיו by ἔντερα with ἐπί and the dative)

I Kg. 1:27 ὑπὲρ τοῦ παιδαρίου τούτου προσηυξάμην

15:35 ὅτι ἐπένθει Σαμουὴλ ἐπὶ Σαούλ...

II Kg. 7:19 καὶ ἐλάλησας ὑπὲρ τοῦ οἴκου...

10:2 παρακαλέσαι αὐτὸν...περὶ τοῦ πατρὸς αὐτοῦ
(the parallel reading in I Chr. 19:2 has על )

24:16 παρεκλήθη Κύριος ἐπὶ τῇ κακίᾳ

IV Kg. 19:20 ἃ προσηύξω πρός με περὶ Σεννα. (Or. על )

Ps. 69:27b καὶ ἐπὶ τὸ ἄλγος τῶν τραυμάτων μου προσέθηκαν

Isa. 37:21 ἃ προσηύξω πρός με περὶ Σεννα. (2 R Or. על )

33 οὕτως λέγει Κύριος ἐπὶ βασιλέα Ἀσσυρίων

Jer. 27(50):1 Λόγος Κυρίου ὃν ἐλάλησεν ἐπὶ Βαβυλῶνα

40:16 ὅτι ψευδῆ σὺ λέγεις ὑπὲρ Ἰσραήλ

Observations-

Of 12, possibly 13, cases, 8 have אל translated by περί (5) or ὑπέρ (3); 4 or 5, by ἐπί. Thus ἐπί shares nearly equally with these two prepositions (which normally are the only ones meaning "concerning") in translating אל where it has the metaphorical denotation "with regard to." ὑπέρ of course carries more precisely the meaning "on account of"; περί and ἐπί, "with regard to" or "with respect to." The prepositions על and אל are used interchangeably in the Masoretic text; there is the possibility that the LXX had על in its Hebrew copy where the Masoretic text reads אל and vice versa. BDB lists some 40 instances where the preposition אל occurs in the MT where analogy would lead one to expect an על or where אל and על

86

are interchangeable, apparently. In every instance where an על would be a better reading than אל the LXX has faithfully rendered the sense ("upon," "over," "against," or "because of"), usually by ἐπί with the genitive or accusative; where the meaning is "unto" there occurs either εἰς or πρός with the accusative. Several of the examples have על and אל in the same sentence with no difference in meaning; in each case the LXX uses the identical preposition as many times as necessary with no regard for the literal reading of the Hebrew. Thus in Jeremiah 43 (36):31 ἐπί and the accusative are used 6 times where על occurs 5 times and אל once; in I Kg. 27:10 κατά and the accusative are used 3 times for 2 עלs and 1 אל; in IV Kg. 8:3 πρός and the accusative, περί and the genitive twice, are found opposite 3 אלs and in 8:5 the same combination for 1 אל and 2 עלs. (Similarly, על occurs where analogy would lead us to expect אל --in these, too, the LXX is concerned to render the sense rather than the letter of the Hebrew.)

Of all the instances where ἐπί and the accusative are found opposite an אל and where BDB thinks an על should be read there is but one with the meaning "concerning," viz. Jer. 40 (33):14 ( אQ): ἐπί and the accusative are found opposite an על and an אל; --and even here the meanings "unto" or "to" are possible.

Thus, examination of the treatment of על and אל in Joshua, Judges, the 4 books of Kingdoms, Jeremiah, Ezekiel (the Psalms have a few examples) indicates that the translators were concerned for the sense and can reasonably be expected to have been indifferent to the occurrence of על as against אל, and vice versa. They seem to translate according to the best meaning, root or derived. Apparently they regarded על and אל as interchangeable in some cases; in others they disregarded the preposition in the MT entirely.

An examination of the use of ἐπί in Attic Greek shows that it has the modified meaning of "so far as regards," "as regards" (Soph. Ant.

899; Eur. Or. 1345; Id. Hec. 514; Xen. Cyr. 1.4, 12; Thuc. 4.28) but all cited cases are of the same form: τό and ἐπί plus a pronoun, viz. τοὐπί με, τὸ ἐπί σε. The following example from the epistle to the Hebrews exhibits ἐπί in the meaning "regarding": 7:13 ἐφ' ὃν γὰρ λέγεται.[1]

Conclusions:

אל derives the significance "with regard to" not from the sense of "upon" or "over" as does על but from the idea of "unto," "toward." In the clause (Mark 9:12, 13) καθὼς γέγραπται ἐπὶ τὸν υἱὸν τοῦ ἀνθρώπου it is hard to tell whether the ἐπί reflects the root meaning of על or אל : if that of על then a Semitism of thought employing a permissible Greek construction is the explanation; if of אל it is a case of coincidence in Semitic and Greek idiom. This coincidence is attested by the examples from the LXX. Although we are keeping in mind that there are examples of אל with the derived meaning "with regard to" and translated as such, inference is all we have for supposing such a derived use was possible Greek. In Hebrews 7:13 the only translation ἐπί and the accusative can sustain is "about." This is a close parallel to γέγραπται ἐπὶ τὸν υἱόν; creases the probability that the ἐπί has the metaphorical significance "with respect to" derived from the root meaning "toward" and thus is equivalent to περί with the genitive.

The preposition "upon" in the locution "have mercy upon"[2] (which was the first item to be examined in this section pages 81ff. ) may

[1] Cf. Heb. 1:8: πρὸς τὸν υἱόν - "concerning the son..."
[2] As to the verb σπλαγχνίζεσθαι being of Semitic coinage (p.85, footnote 1): the noun σπλάγχνον in the metaphorical sense appears in classical literature; it denotes anger, anxiety, but not pity. The earliest example of the last-named meaning in secular literature is in a papyrus of the first century B.C.: BGU 1139, 17 Διὸ ἀξιοῦμέν σε τὸν πάντων σωτῆρα...ὑπὲρ σπλάγχνου ("for pity's sake") (5a). It is impossible to say anything about the origin of the locution from this meager attestation; it might reasonably be assumed that the meaning "to pity" developed within the koine but subject to what influence it is hard to say.

be contained in the verb (or the verb may merely mean "to feel compassion") as was the case in the citation from the LXX (Ps. 103: 13); if this is true the ἐπί in the Markan passages will carry the "unto-with respect to" signification. Two of the passages are treated by Matthew as follows: The ἐπ'αὐτούς of 6:34 is paralleled by ἐπ'αὐτοῖς ; the ἐπὶ τὸν ὄχλον of 8:2 by ἐπὶ τὸν ὄχλον. But Matthew also has the construction with περί (9:36): ἐσπλαγχνίσθη περὶ αὐτῶν as well as the genitive alone (18:27). We can scarcely say that this evangelist makes indifferent use of the accusative with ἐπί, the dative with ἐπί, and the genitive with περί ; yet the fact that he follows Mark in using ἐπί and the accusative with σπλαγχνίζεσθαι in one instance (parallel to 8:2) must mean that, preferring to use περί with the genitive,[1] he did not feel that Greek usage was strained by employing ἐπί and the accusative to denote the end-object of an action.[2] Thus we again arrive at the "unto-with respect to" understanding of ἐπί with the accusative. Paul uses εἰς and the accusative to convey the "unto" signification with the noun σπλάγχνα :

II Cor. 8:15 τὰ σπλάγχνα αὐτοῦ περισσοτέρως εἰς ὑμᾶς ἐστίν. In addition, two examples are found in the Shepherd of Hermas:

Mandata IV 3, 5 πολύσπλαγχνος οὖν ὢν ὁ κύριος ἐσπλαγχνίσθη ἐπὶ τὴν π.

Sim. IX 24, 2 καὶ πάντοτε σπλάγχνον ἔχοντες ἐπὶ πάντα ἄνθρωπον...

Having said this, we may note the possibility that σπλαγχνίζεσθαι ἐπί... plus the accusative is a literal rendering of a late biblical Hebrew (or Aramaic) locution in which the preposition in the verb

---

[1] That is, when he is not following Mark.
[2] Lk. 7:13 reads ὁ κύριος ἐσπλαγχνίσθη ἐπ'αὐτήν (ABCD- τῇ ; ℵ 13-69-346 33 669* 700- τήν ) where the change to the dative may reflect a difficulty in reading the accusative.

רחם (Ar. רחב ) is separately expressed. No set of examples which would give probability to such a supposition is at hand, however; and ἐπί and the accusative used with σπλαγχνίζεσθαι can be understood as carrying the permissible Attic meaning of "with respect to."[1] Thus, "ἐπί and the accusative used where περί and the genitive would be proper" is probably to be classed as a coincidence of Semitic and Greek idiom.[2]

### 10. The use of the positive degree of the adjective for the comparative (I.6.A)

The καλόν of Mark 9:43, 45, and 47 may be an example of the positive degree of the adjective used for the comparative; however, it may be an example of the use of ἤ with the positive degree of the adjective where the ἤ nas adversative, and not comparing force:

Herod. 9, 26 οὕτω ὦν δίκαιόν ( sc. ἐστι) ἡμέας ἔχειν τὸ ἕτερον κέρας ἤπερ Ἀθηναίους here "..us, rather than the A." This is not a case of δίκαιον standing for δικαιότερον (which scarcely ever appears) with the idea of comparison conveyed entirely by the particle ἤ. Another example of this use is found in II Macc. 7:2 ἕτοιμοι γὰρ ἀποθνήσκειν ἐσμὲν ἢ πατρῴους νόμους παραβαίνειν not "We are better prepared to...and not to...."[3] Concerning Mark 9:45 Swete observes (op.cit.ad.loc.): "ἀπελθεῖν and εἰσελθεῖν are in marked contrast" -- so that comparison between them is not signified so much as the emphasizing of the one to the exclusion of the

---

[1] Cf. the Latin: misercordia pro nobis 'mercy on us.'
[2] The verb σπλαγχνίζεσθαι can be translated "to feel pity" or "to feel pity for": Mt. 18:27 and Lk. 15:20 have σπλαγχνίζεσθαι in a participial form which may share an accusative with the main verb; Mt. 20:34, Mk. 1:41 and Lk. 10:43 have simply σπλαγχνισθείς. These would indicate that "feeling compassion" with no addition of a preposition is all that the verb means.
[3] Mayser cites a passage (GGP II i, 54) where ἤ appears with the superlative, not as a comparing, but as an adversative particle: Philemon frg. 109 (Mein. com. fr. IV, 63) θανεῖν ἄριστόν ἐστιν ἢ ζῆν ἀθλίως.

other: it is good to enter into life...rather than to go away into gehenna. To be sure, entering into life and going into gehenna are not the only contraposed ideas: "maimed" and "with two hands" constitute a counter contrast, the former offsetting the desirability of entering into life and the other mitigating going to gehenna. However, one could hardly say: it is good to enter into gehenna...better, into life. The meaning seems to be: It is well to enter into life, even though maimed, than (= and not to) with two hands to go into gehenna.

Examples of a positive degree of the adjective used as a comparative follow:

Gen. 49:12 λευκοὶ οἱ ὀδόντες αὐτοῦ ἢ γάλα
       ולבן־שנים מחלב    (comparison)

Dt. 7:17 πολὺ τὸ ἔθνος τοῦτο ἢ ἐγώ
       רבים הגוים האלה ממני  (comparison or contrast)

Hos. 2:9 ὅτι καλῶς μοι ἦν τότε ἢ νῦν
       כי טוב לי אז מעתה  (comparison or contrast)

Jon. 4:3 ὅτι καλὸν τὸ ἀποθανεῖν με ἢ ζῆν με
       כי טוב מותי מחיי   ("better")

Lam. 4:9 καλοὶ ἦσαν οἱ τραυματίαι ῥομφαίας ἢ οἱ τραυματίαι λιμοῦ
       טובים היו חללי־חרב מחללי רעב

Probably none of these examples are of the type: it is good...than (and not)..., although the ἢ of Hos. 2:9 may be taken as adversative.

There are cases (probably a majority) where the Greek does not adhere to the Hebrew usage:

Gen. 29:19 Βέλτιον δοῦναί με αὐτὴν σοὶ ἢ δοῦναί με αὐτὴν ἑτέρῳ ἀνδρί
       טוב תתי אתה לך מתתי אתה לאיש אחר

Ex. 14:12 κρεῖσσον γὰρ ἡμᾶς δουλεύειν τοῖς Αἰγυπτίοις ἢ ἀποθνῄσκειν

כי טוב לנו עבד את־מצרים ממתנו במדבר

The use of the positive degree of the adjective for the comparative is not a consistent feature of the LXX. Where it is found it is probably based on the Hebrew manner of expressing comparison by the adjective and the preposition although no point-to-point correspondence between Greek and Hebrew is at hand.

Conclusions:

If the ἤ of Mark 9:43, 45, and 47 is adversative, the locutions in which it appears do not ask for explanation. If it is to be understood as a particle of comparison, the καλόν may be explained as the use of the positive degree of the adjective for the comparative based upon a Semitic usage. The more recent translators (Weymouth, Goodspeed, Torrey, Moffat, Cambridge Bible, and RSV) take the καλόν of Mark 9:43, 45, and 47 as equivalent to a comparative degree of the adjective; the older (Gould, ICC, Swete, RV) translate it as "good" or "well" and understand ἤ as having adversative force. It must be conceded that "better...than..." is a more facile rendering of καλόν...ἤ than "good(well)...rather than..." such a consideration may account for the treatment of the passage by some of the more recent translators. However, the interpretation "good...rather than..." probably states correctly the relation between "going into life" and "going away into gehenna," as we have shown.

11. The use of the cardinal for the ordinal (I.7.A.1

An examination of the passages where εἷς appears in the LXX yields the following data:

1. ὁ εἷς appears frequently coupled with ὁ δεύτερος translating the Hebrew האחד and השני :[1] this is not a clearcut case of

---

[1] ὁ εἷς-ὁ ἕτερος translate the same set of Hebrew words in Dan. 8:3.

εἷς being used as the equivalent of an ordinal--the sense is not "the first (the former)...the second (the latter)..." but "(the)one...the other..." Such is the case in Gen. 4:19; Exod. 1:15; 25:11 (12), 31 (32); Num. 11:26; Ruth 1:4; I Kngd. 1:2; II Kngd. 4:2; III Kngd. 7:4, 5, 7. ὁ εἷς...ὁ ἄλλος render האחד...האחד in Gen. 42:32; I Kngd. 14:4, 5; III Kngd. 18:23; Zech. 11:7; Jer. 24:2. ὁ εἷς...ὁ δεύτερος render האחת(ה)...אחרת in Ezek. 41:24.

The use of εἷς with δεύτερος corresponding to the Latin unus ...alter, is found in late Greek writers (after 50 B.C.). Latin uses not only unus with alter regularly but even unus, alter, and tertius at times:

Cic. Clu. 64.178 unum, alterum, tertium annum Sassia quiescebat. This may, of course, be "the first, the second the third year etc." but more likely is it "one year, another, a third year etc." An ordinal is not called for in designating the first and second years because the writer (speaker) deliberately avoids (for rhetorical effect) denoting a series at the beginning of the clause Greek may have had a parallel and somewhat ambiguous way of thinking of εἷς as "(the)one-the first"; if such were the case, it would account for the use of εἷς with δεύτερος in rendering the Hebrew האחד and השני.

2. εἷς with the article used as an ordinal appears in Gen. 2:11 where it means "the first (of four)" and in a Greek addition to the title of Ps. 23 (24).

3. εἷς without the article, used as an ordinal, is restricted to the phrase (ἡμέρᾳ)μιᾷ τοῦ μηνός which occurs in the following passages: Gen. 8:13; Exod. 39:12; 40:2; Lev. 23:24; Num. 1:1, 18; 29:1: 33:38; Dt. 1:3; II Esd. (Ezra) 3:6; 7:9; 10:16 ( א A), 17; 18:2 (Neh. 8:2); Hag. 1:1; Ezek. 26:1; 29:17; 31:1; 32:1; 45:18.[1]

---

[1]In such late passages as the Hebrew of Ezra 3:6, 10:17, Neh. 8:2, where יום is inserted (G-K 457), the original is followed by the Greek and a ἡμέρα is included.

4. The Greek does not follow the Hebrew in rendering a cardinal by a cardinal for numbers other than one, viz.

Lev. 33:32   תשעה   ἐνάτης
IV Kngd. 25:8   בשבעה לחדש   ἑβδόμῃ τοῦ μηνός
II Chr. 29:17   בשמנה   ὀγδόῃ
Ez. 1:1   חמשה   πέμπτῃ
    30:20   בשבעה לחדש   ἑβδόμῃ τοῦ μηνός
Zech. 7:1   ארבע(with שנת)   τετάρτῳ

5. πρῶτος translates אחד with dates 9 times; once it means "the first (of three)" (possibly "the one..."): Gen. 8:5; II Chr. 29:17; 36:22; II Esd. 1:1; 7:9; Dan 1:21 (Theod. has ἑνός); 9:1 (Theod. πρώτῳ); 11:1; and Job 42:14. In addition it translates חדה 3 times: II Esd. 5:13; 6:3; Dan. 7:1.

6. Exod. 12:18 has the form ἡμέρας μιᾶς καὶ εἰκάδος τοῦ μην. (this usage is not the same as ἡμέρας μιᾶς καὶ εἰκοστῆς as Moulton remarks [Proleg. 96]): literally, it is not "one-and-twentieth" but "one and the twentieth,"[1] indicating that εἷς is a more or less fixed equivalent for אחד where it occurs with יום --even where a compound ordinal is to be translated. The identical Hebrew ordinal is rendered in I Chr. 24:17 by ὁ εἷς καὶ εἰκοστός and in I Chr. 25:28 by ὁ εἰκοστὸς (A adds καὶ) πρῶτος with κλῆρος; in III Kngd. 16:23 the Hebrew ordinal for "thirty-first," identical in form with that of Exod. 12:18, is translated by τριακοστῷ καὶ πρώτῳ with ἔτει. With the exception of II Chr. 29:17 and II Esd. 7:9, πρῶτος is not used to denote the day of the month; although, as we have seen (observation 5), it is used 12 times (9 for אחד and 3 for חדה ) where dates are concerned.[2]

---

[1] Cf. Esther 8:9 τρίτῃ καὶ εἰκάδι τοῦ αὐτοῦ ἔτους   Heb. בשלושה ועשרים.

[2] All examples of πρῶτος rendering from the Aramaic occur with ἔτει.

Conclusions:

Consideration of observations 3 and 6 establishes the fact that εἷς without the article and used as an ordinal is almost completely limited to designating the first day of the month. The presumption is that (ἡμέρας) μιᾶς originating as literal translation, was preferred to (ἡμέρας) πρώτης as the equivalent to the Hebrew אחד יום;[1] and that extension of the preference to ordinals used with words other than ἡμέρα seemingly encountered resistance-- such resistance not being complete, as Gen. 2:11, observation 2, testifies. Extension beyond the number one of the practice of a Greek cardinal for a Hebrew cardinal where the latter is used for an ordinal (numbers 2-10 only) is not found (see observation 4).

When we examine the use of εἷς as an ordinal in the NT we find that, outside of the gospels, it occurs in the following passages:

Acts 20:7 ἐν τῇ μιᾷ σαββάτων

I Cor. 16:2 κατὰ μίαν σαββάτου

Titus 3:10 αἱρετικὸν ἄνθρωπον μετὰ μίαν καὶ δευτέραν νουθεσίαν παραιτοῦ

Rev. 9:12 ἡ οὐαὶ ἡ μία ἀπῆλθεν

From the two former we infer that the phrase ἡ μία(ἡμέρα) σαββάτων (-του) was a part of the vocabulary of Luke and Paul; that εἷς had some equivalence to πρῶτος is shown by I Cor. 16:2 and Titus 3:10, where translation cannot be advanced to account for its presence. The latter of these two may, of course, be translated "one...a second..." after the fashion noted in observation 1; the former of the two shows us that we can be fairly sure of the equivalence of εἷς for πρῶτος used with a day of the week or month. Accordingly, our conclusion is that the phrase τῇ μιᾷ of Mark 16:2 is a fixed phrase already

---

[1]Cf. Joseph. Ant. I.1 (i 29): αὕτη μὲν ἂν εἴη πρώτη ἡμέρα, Μωϋσῆς δ'αὐτὴν μίαν εἶπεν.

available in Greek to the evangelist at the time his gospel was written and is to be understood, in all probability, as a biblicism.

12. Duplication as a distributive designation (I.7.B)

The repetition of a cardinal number (and of certain words other than numerals) as a distributive designation was shown to have some Attic precedent but no contemporary attestation in the papyri (page 35). Modern Greek has a kind of parallel in such usages as the following:

περατῶ τὸ γιαλὸ γιαλό
("I kept walking along the shore," literally "shore by shore.")

ἐπερίμενα ὧρες ὧρες (cited by Dieterich, Untersuchungen, 188)
("I waited for hours," literally "hour by hour.")

Thackeray states that duplication as a distributive designation is a case where "the usage of the Hebrew and the Greek vernacular coincide" (Gram. OT Gr. I, 54). Vergote (Phil. Studien vol. 6, 104), with the κατα δύο δύο of P. Ox. 886 (IIIp) and the δύο δύο of Gen. 6:19 in mind, cites Coptic parallels with a rendering of the phrase καθ' ἕνα of I Cor. 14:3 (in a Coptic version of the New Testament) by the preposition and the numeral repeated (the εἷς κατα εἷς of Mark 14:19 is rendered in the same fashion as the καθ'ἕνα of I Cor. 14:3).

The distributive idea is expressed in the LXX as follows:

1. Gen. 6:19; 7:2, 3, 9, 15; Ex. 8:14, by duplication.

2. III Kngd. 18:13 has ἀνὰ πεντήκοντα for the Hebrew
חמשים חמשים

3. II Kngd. 21:20 has ἓξ καὶ ἕξ for the Hebrew שש ושש

(Aside from numerals)

4. Gen. 32:17 has ποίμνιον κατὰ μόνας for the Hebrew
עדר עדר לבדו

Exod. 36:4 has ἕκαστος for the Hebrew איש־איש

Dt. 15:20 has ἐνιαυτὸν ἐξ ἐνιαυτοῦ for the Hebrew
שנה בשנה

I Kngd. 1:7 has ἐνιαυτὸν κατ' ἐνιαυτόν for the Hebrew שנה בשנה

5. Lev. 24:8 τῇ ἡμέρᾳ τῶν σαββάτων
ביום השבת ביום השבת

I Chr. 9:27 τὸ πρωΐ πρωΐ ( ℵ om 2nd πρωΐ )   לבקר לבקר
Ps. 62(63):14 εἰς τὰς πρωίας   לבקרים[1]
Job 7:18 ἕως τὸ πρωΐ καὶ εἰς ἀνάπαυσιν
    לבקרם לרגעים[1]
Esther 8:9 κατὰ χώραν καὶ χώραν   מדינה ומדינה

6. Nu. 24:1 κατὰ εἰωθός for the Hebrew בפעם בפעם (for the same Hebrew phrase ὡς ἅπαξ καὶ ἅπαξ is found in Ju. 16:20 ( καθὼς ἀεί-A ), 20:31; I Kngd. 3:10, 20:25.

7. Ezra 10:14 πρεσβύτερος πόλεως   זקני־עיר ועיר

8. I Chr. 26:13 εἰς πυλῶνα καὶ πυλῶνα   לשער ושער

The compound expression of the type found in P. Ox. 886 κατὰ δύο δύο is found in the translation of מעט מעט by κατὰ μικρὸν μικρόν in Dt. 7:22; of משפחות משפחות by κατὰ φυλὰς φυλάς in Zech. 12:13; of שנה בשנה by κατ' ἐνιαυτὸν ἐνιαυτόν in I Kngd. 7:16; whereas ἐνιαυτὸν κατ' ἐνιαυτόν renders שנה בשנה in I Kngd. 1:7, II Chr. 24:5, II Esd. (Neh.) 20(10) 34(35), 35(36), and in Dt. 14:22. The Greek expression of the type ἡμέραν ἐξ ἡμέρας renders יום יום in Gen. 39:10, יום ביום in I Chr. 12:12, שנה בשנה (ἐνιαυτὸν ἐξ ἐνιαυτοῦ) in Dt. 15:20. In these examples the Greek is without any precise correspondence to the Hebrew original. The Greek expression of the type κατ' ἐνιαυτόν renders שנה בשנה in III Kngd. 5:11 (25) and Zech. 14:16, בשנה in II Esd.(Neh.) 20(10):32 (33), ( יום יום in Prov. 8:30, 34 by καθ' ἡμέραν ). The foregoing observations establish the fact that Hebrew expressed the distributive various-

---

[1] The sense of the Hebrew is evidently not understood.

ly and Greek did likewise but no correlation is discovered except a possible preference for the form ἐνιαυτὸν κατ'ἐνιαυτόν where the preposition ב occurs. Such a type as κατὰ φυλὰς φυλάς may be used to do justice to both Greek and Hebrew syntax. Such a type as ἐνιαυτὸν κατ'ἐνιαυτόν also has some point-to-point correspondence to a Hebrew phrase--which correspondence is not present when it translates שנה שנה. The following grouping shows that the types ἐνιαυτὸν κατ'ἐνιαυτόν, κατ'ἐνιαυτὸν ἐνιαυτόν and κατ'ἐνιαυτόν were all acceptable ways of denoting the distributive in Greek:

ἐνιαυτὸν κατ'ἐνιαυτόν    κατ'ἐνιαυτὸν ἐνιαυτόν    κατ'ἐνιαυτόν

    Dt. 14:22           Dt. 7:22           III Kngd. 5:11
    I Kngd. 1:7         I Kngd. 7:16      Zech. 14:16
    Ps. 67:19           III Kngd. 10:28   II Esd. 20:32
    II Chr. 24:5        Zech. 12:13
    II Esd. 20:34       II Chr. 9:24

The considerations just put forward do little more than establish a likelihood that repetition (of the numeral and of other words) as a distributive designation was possible vernacular Greek; the Greek usages exhibit some independence of (although modelled upon) the Hebrew, and thus they give us to suppose that they had a currency of their own.

13. The redundant pronoun (I.8.A.1)

The following examples of the treatment of the Hebrew relative and retrospective pronoun in the LXX have been selected at random:

Gen. 45:4    אני יוסף אשר מכרתם אתי
Ἐγώ εἰμι Ἰωσήφ...ὃν ἀπέδοσθε εἰς Αἴγ.

Ps. 1:4    כמץ אשר תדפנו רוח
ὁ χνοῦς ὃν ἐκριπτεῖ ὁ ἄνεμος

Gen. 21:2    למועד אשר דבר אתו אלהים
εἰς τὸν καιρὸν καθὰ ἐλάλησεν αὐτῷ κύριος

Exod. 6:5    בני ישראל אשר מצרים מעבדים אתם
τῶν υἱῶν Ἰσραήλ, ὃν Α. καταδουλοῦνται αὐτούς

Dt. 28:49   גוי אשר לא-תשמע לשונו
ἔθνος ὃ οὐκ ἀκούσῃ τῆς φωνῆς αὐτοῦ   ( οὗ-AF)

Gen. 24:3   הכנעני אשר אנכי יושב בקרבו
μεθ'ὧν ἐγὼ οἰκῶ μετ'αὐτῶν

38:25   לאיש אשר אלה לו
ἐκ τοῦ ἀνθρώπου οὗτινος ταῦτά ἐστιν

Exod. 4:17   בידך אשר תעשה בו
ἐν ᾗ ποιήσεις ἐν αὐτῇ τὰ κτλ.

Gen. 28:13   הארץ אשר אתה שכב עליה לך אתננה
ἡ γῆ ἐφ'ἧς σὺ καθεύδεις ἐπ'αὐτῆς, σοὶ δώσω αὐτήν

Num. 22:30   אתנך אשר רכבת עלי
ἡ ὄνος σου ἐφ'ἧς ἐπέβαινες ἀπὸ νεότητος κτλ.

Dt. 1:22 (a)   הדרך אשר נעלה-בה
τὴν ὁδὸν δι'ἧς ἀναβησόμεθα ἐν αὐτῇ

(b)   הערים אשר נבא עלהן
τὰς πόλεις εἰς ἃς εἰσπορευσόμεθα εἰς αὐτάς

Ruth 2:12   יהוה...אשר באת לחסות תחת-כנפיו
παρὰ Κυρίου...πρὸς ὃν ἦλθες πεποιθέναι ὑπὸ τὰς πτέρυγας αὐτοῦ

Isa. 1:21   צדק ילין בה
ἐν ᾗ δικαιοσύνη ἐκοιμήθη ἐν αὐτῇ

Lev. 16:32 (Gk. only) ἱλάσκεται ὁ ἱερεύς, ὃν ἂν χρίσωσιν αὐτόν

Num. 17:5 (MT-17:20) καὶ ἔσται ὁ ἄνθρωπος ὃν ἐὰν ἐκλέξομαι αὐτόν

Jos. 3:4 ἵν'ἐπίστησθε τὴν ὁδὸν ἣν πορεύεσθε αὐτήν

Ruth 3:2 Βόος...οὗ ἧς μετὰ τῶν κορασίων αὐτοῦ

III Kngd. 11:34 διὰ Δαυεὶδ...ὃν ἐξελεξάμην αὐτόν

IV Kngd. 19:4 Ῥαψάκου, ὃν ἀπέστειλεν αὐτὸν βασιλεὺς Ἀσσυρίων ὁ κύριος αὐτοῦ

II Esd. 18 (Neh. 8):10 ὅτι συνῆκαν ἐν τοῖς λόγοις οἷς ἐγνώρισεν αὐτοῖς

Ps. 39:5 μακάριος ἀνὴρ οὗ ἐστιν τὸ ὄνομα Κυρίου ἐλπὶς αὐτοῦ

Observations-

1. Of the 22 examples selected at random 5 have no redundant pronoun in the Greek (Gen. 45:4; Ps. 1:4; Gen. 21:2; 38:25; Num. 22:30).

2. 13 have constructions in which a personal pronoun is found in the same clause and regimen as the relative pronoun (Gen. 24:3; 28:13; Exod. 4:17; Dt. 1:22b; Lev. 16:32; Num. 17:5; Jos. 3:4; Ruth 3:2; III Kngd. 11:34; IV Kngd. 19:4; II Esd.18:10; Ps. 39:5; Isa. 1:21.

3. 1 has a duplication of pronoun where there is but one in the original (Isa. 1:21).

4. In 5 instances literal adherence to the Hebrew text may be responsible for the use made of the pronoun. In one of these (Exod.6:5) the relative pronoun does not agree with its antecedent in number (unless ὄν refers to Ἰσραήλ ); in another (Dt. 28:49) the relative pronoun may owe its case to assimilation with its antecedent--which assimilation would be unusual--or indifference to case usage in the clause in which the relative occurs may be responsible (the correction in AF suggests that this latter is the case); in a third (Gen. 28:13) the word order and the case usage are the same as the Hebrew. A fourth (Dt. 1:22a) and a fifth (Ruth 2:12) exhibit equivalents for the resumptive pronoun in cases different from those of the relative pronoun at the beginning of the clause. The presumption about two of these instances (Exod. 6:5 and Dt. 18:49) is that the relative pronoun is little more than a word indicating that a subordinate clause follows, and that nothing of the exact relation referred to in the preceding sentence found in the δι' ἧς of Dt. 1:22a and the πρὸς ὄν of Ruth 2:12 are corrected by the ἐν αὐτῇ and the αὐτοῦ.

The construction mentioned in observation 2 is not unlike that of P. Ox. 117 and 1070. Classical practice when a relative clause was continued by a clause coördinate with it, was to abandon the relative construction in the second clause and to replace the relative by a personal or demonstrative pronoun. Driver cites the following as an extension of this practice (Orig. Lang. 4):

Soph. Philoct. 315 (MSS) τοιαῦτα Ἀτρεῖδαί μ'ῆτε Ὀδυσσέως βία ὦ παῖ, δεδράκασ''; οἷς Ὀλύμπιοι θεοὶ δοῖέν ποτ'αὐτοῖς ἀντίποιν'ἐμοῦ παθεῖν

Callim. Epigr. 43 ὧν ὁ μὲν αὐτῶν

Anth. Pal. ὧν ὁ μὲν ὑμῶν

Additional examples are:

Hyperid. Euxen. 3 ὧν οὐδεμ[ία]δήπου τῶν αἰτι[ῶ]ν τούτων οὐδὲν κοινωνεῖ τῶ[ι] εἰσαγγελτικῶι νόμωι

Pausanias 2.4.7 ὧν τὴν μὲν Πελαγίαν τὴν δὲ Αἰγυπτίαν αὐτῶν ἐπονομάζουσιν

Xen. Cyr. 1.4.19 οἱ ἢν ἐπ'ἐκείνους ἡμεῖς ἐλαύνωμεν, ὑποτεμοῦνται πάλιν ἡμᾶς ἐκεῖνοι

Vergote (op.cit.VI, 104) states that Coptic has numerous examples of the usage of the type exhibited in the examples given above. Regarding the type found in observation 2 Thackeray says (op.cit.46): "...the fact that it (our construction) is found in an original Greek work such as II Maccabees (12:27) ἐν ᾗ...ἐν αὐτῇ and a paraphrase such as I Esdras (3:5, 9; 4:54 63; 6:32) is sufficient to warrant its presence in the koine."

The examples referred to under observation 2 have constructions that are passable Greek: in 16 cases adherence to the Hebrew apparently dictates the use of an uncommon Greek construction; in 1 case (Gen. 28:13--mentioned under observations 2 and 4) the word order is that of the Hebrew and the case usage is both Hebrew and Greek; for the relative and personal pronouns of a fifth (Isa. 1:21) there is only a personal pronoun in the Hebrew. Leaving out of account the five examples where אשר is followed by the retrospective pronoun but where the Greek rendering has no redundant pronoun, and the one example of a duplicated pronoun in the Greek where there is but one in the original, we have three translation types:

(1) Un-Greek usage, exhibiting a word-for-word adherence to the Hebrew (Exod. 6:5; Dt. 28:49);

(2) Passable Greek, for the uncommon form of which adherence to the Hebrew is responsible (Gen. 24:3; 28:13; Exod. 4:17; Dt. 1:22b; Lev. 16:32; Num. 17:5; Jos. 3:4; Ruth 3:2; III Kngd. 11:34; IV Kngd. 19:4; II Esdras 18:10; Ps. 39:5);

(3) Passable Greek, but exhibiting a word-for-word adherence to the Hebrew (Gen. 18:13; Dt. 1:22a; Ruth 2:12).

The example(s)[1] in Mark of a redundant personal pronoun occurring in a clause introduced by a relative pronoun is (are) of type (2): passable Greek for cases of which found in the LXX adherence to the Hebrew original is apparently responsible. Type (2), however, is found in other parts of the New Testament:

Acts 15:17 πάντα τὰ ἔθνη, ἐφ' οὕς ἐπικέκληται τὸ ὄνομά μου ἐπ' αὐτούς  (LXX of Amos 9:12)

Philemon 12 Ὀνήσιμον...ὃν ἀνέπεμψά σοι αὐτόν

Outside of the New Testament:

I Clement 21:9 οὗ ἡ πνοὴ αὐτοῦ

Philemon and I Clement weigh heavily against the probability that any degree of adherence to a Semitic original is responsible for type (2) in Mark. The question is not so nicely poised as to be decided by two examples, however. On the one side there are these considerations: (1)

---

[1]As noted before (page 38, note 1), the MS support for αὐτῆς in 7:25 is not very strong.

5 of 22 examples selected at random have no redundant pronoun, (2) there is one case of a redundant pronoun in the Greek where none in the Hebrew, and (3) the usage is found in passages that are free from Semitic influence. On the other side there is this: there are fourteen examples of a redundant pronoun in translation Greek, all of which may be, and almost certainly one (Dt. 28:49) of which is, due to the influence of the Hebrew. The status of the locution (type 2 ) is this:

1. It is passable Greek.

2. Its presence in a piece of writing does not indicate whether translation or original composition is to be posited: both have been found to account for it.

3. It may be a biblicism.

Thus, the locution takes a place with those of the impersonal third plural (page 70) and of the distributive singular (page 73) (although the presence of translation is even less necessary a supposition here than in the case of the third plural); as a translation phenomenon, it does not by itself unfailingly indicate translation.

The treatment of a resumptive word in the LXX is somewhat the same as that of the retrospective pronoun:

Gen. 41:19   לא־ראתי כהנה בכל־ארץ מצרים
οἵας οὐκ εἶδον τοιαύτας ἐν ὅλῃ Αἰ.
(οἵας is here a connective supplied by the Greek)

cf. Exod. 9:24   אשר לא־היה כמהו
ἥτις τοιαύτη οὐ γέγονεν

and 11:6   אשר כמהו לא נהיתה
ἥτις τοιαύτη οὐ γέγονεν

Gen. 3:23   אשר...משם   ἐξ ἧς ἐλήμφθη

13:3   אשר...שם   τοῦ τρόπου οὗ ἦν ἡ σκηνὴ αὐτοῦ

4   אשר...שם   οὐ ἐποίησεν ἐκεῖ τὴν σκηνήν

Exod. 21:13   אשר...שמה   τόπον οὗ φεύξεται ἐκεῖ ὁ

φονεύσας

The only other passage where οἷος...τοιοῦτος occurs in the LXX is Sirach 49:14: οὐδὲ εἷς ἐκτίσθη οἷος Ἐνὼχ τοιοῦτος ἐπὶ τῆς γῆς ( ℵ A read, probably as a correction, ἐπὶ τῆς γῆς τοιοῦτος οἷος Ἐνώχ ).

οἷος...τοιοῦτος is not due to a literal rendering of a Hebrew locution- the parallel expression ἥτις...τοιαύτη is, apparently. The expression of Mark 13:19,[1] θλῖψις, οἵα οὐ γέγονεν τοιαύτη does not occur, as Hawkins notes (op.cit. 134),"in Dan. 12:1 (either LXX or Theodotion) which is here being referred to." οἷα οὐκ ἐγενήθη in Dan. 9:12 (LXX- γέγονεν Θ) and 12:1 translates the Hebrew אשר לא־נ(התה‎- 9:12)נהיתה . It seems quite probable that οἷος...τοιοῦτος occurring in a single clause is an example of redundancy of expression that may be expected in such non-literary writing as we have found Mark to be.

The redundant words in the locutions of Mark 6:10 ὅπου ἐὰν εἰσέλθητε εἰς οἰκίαν- ἐκεῖ μένετε ἕως ἂν ἐξέλθητε ἐκεῖθεν may be considered as added and explanatory ("into a house," "from that place") or they may be a patois influenced by Semitic usage. The examples taken from the LXX are as indecisive as were those considered in connection with the redundant pronoun, and a canvass of all the instances where שם is rendered in the Greek probably would contribute little more toward deciding the question. οὗ...ἐκεῖ...or ὅπου...εἰς οἰκίαν is not fundamentally dissimilar to a citation from Xenophon in which we find (Cyr. 1.4.19) οἳ...ἐκεῖνοι --the pleonasm being that of the adjective rather than the adverb. The probability is that the locutions are vernacular Greek containing a somewhat redundant addition of a prepositional phrase in one case and of an adverb in the other.

[1] The οἷα...οὕτως of Mk. 9:3 is to be noted as well.

## 14. The use of οὐ(μη)...πᾶς for οὐδείς (I.8.A.2)

Of ten examples of Greek equivalents in the LXX for the Hebrew כל...לא, 5 have οὐ(μή)...πᾶς and 5 have οὐ (plus μή occasionally)... οὐδέν. Winer (<u>Gram</u>. <u>NT Gr</u>.215) cites ten examples where the Greek follows the Hebrew in rendering כל...לא by οὐ(μή)...πᾶς and five where it does not.[1] Howard admits (<u>op. cit</u>.434) οὐ(μή)...πᾶς is a Hebraism; Winer is quoted: "...this Hebraism should in strictness be limited to the expression οὐ(μή)...πᾶς ; for in sentences with πᾶς ...οὐ(μή) there is usually nothing that is alien to Greek usage." The phrase of Mark 13:20, οὐκ...πᾶσα σάρξ , is found outside of that gospel: Matthew (parallel to Mark 13:20), Ro. 3:20, I Cor. 1:29, Gal. 2:16. οὐ(μή)...πᾶς is used as an equivalent for οὐδείς in the Synoptics, Acts, Revelation, John, I John, the Pauline epistles, II Peter, the Didache, and the Protevangelium Jacobi.

It seems that what we have in the locution of Mark 13:20 is really two biblicisms or one biblicism and one Hebraism. The Hebraic "all flesh" is undoubtedly in mind in the quotations from Romans, Galatians, and Mark (parallel in Matthew). The reading in these three is not a quotation from the LXX, but there is a distinct resemblance to Ps. 142 (Heb. 143) 2; the reading there, however, is not πᾶσα σάρξ but πᾶς ζῶν (some MSS read πᾶσα σάρξ even here). In the passages from Galatians and Romans what we have is a quotation from the LXX with a substitution of πᾶσα σάρξ , a biblicism,[2] for πᾶς ζῶν. Similarly, it would seem that πᾶσα σάρξ in the quotation from Mark 13:20 is a biblicism and οὐ...πᾶσα a biblicism or a Hebraism. The argument for the latter of these two apparently rests upon such evidence as that from

---

[1] Theodotion uses παντὸς...οὐ in translating Dan. 11:37 which has no כל.

[2] πᾶσα σάρξ occurs in I Cor. 15:39.

105

P. Ryl. ii 213.[1] To tip the argument for a Hebraism with one quotation from a papyrus of the first part of the second century A.D. is precarious, of course; yet it is difficult to ignore it. The papyrus seems to be out of the range of LXX influence.

We may conclude that at least the phrase οὐ...πᾶσα(σάρξ) with which we have to do in Mark 13:20, is probably a Hebraism, mediated to the evangelist by the LXX.

15. ἔρχεται as equivalent to the passive of φέρω (I.9.A.1)

Allen (Exp. Times, xiii 1892, 330) says: "ἔρχεται (Mk. 4:21) is a mistranslation of the Aphel or Ittaphal of אתא = 'bring' or 'be brought'." If we have in ἔρχεται a mistranslation of the Aphel it seems likely that the Aphel was in turn read for what was originally a passive. The hypothesis of mistranslation is plausible: the passage is a saying of Jesus and that presupposes translation somewhere along the line. ἔρχεται is followed by a passive τεθῇ ; when it is recalled that the verb "come" is used in Aramaic in the Aphel with the meaning "bring" and inasmuch as active and passive forms of this verb are easily confused it is readily seen that the verb which ἔρχεται translates may well have been passive, as the sense requires.

16. The periphrasis of the imperfect (and future) (I.9.B.2)

Burney (Aram.Or. Fourth Gosp. 92f), in an effort to show that the Greek imperfect in John's gospel points to the Aramaic use of the participle coupled with the substantive verb, lists 29 cases from the book of Daniel where the Aramaic has a coupling of a participle and substantive verb to describe past events: of 15 equivalents in the LXX, 11 have an

---

[1] In this papyrus a certain Hieracion of Letopolis, beekeeper, complains of unjust treatment from persons μὴ ἔχοντας πᾶν πρᾶγμα πρὸς ἐμέ (133p)- the document is quite ungrammatical and shows no marks of Semitic provenance.

imperfect, 2 a perfect, 1 a participle, and 1 an analytic tense (θεω-ρῶν ἤμην); of 28 equivalents in Theodotion, 23 have an imperfect, 4 an analytic tense, and 1 a kind of paraphrase ( ἦν[no other verb form in the Greek]...ὑπέρ for על מתנצח היה).

The following are examples of Greek analytic tenses together with the Hebrew and Aramaic which they translate:

| | LXX | Theodotion | Hebrew |
|---|---|---|---|
| Dan. 1:16 | ἦν ἀναιρού-μενος ἀντιεδίδου | ἐγένετο ἀναιρού-μενος ἐδίδου | ויהי...נשא ונתן |
| | | | Aramaic |
| 2:43 | οὐκ ἔσονται ὁμονοοῦντες | προσκολλώμενοι | לא להון דבקים |
| 6:18(19) | ἦν λυπού-μενος | οὐκ ἦν ἁπτό-μενος | אין נוגע |
| 7:13 | ἤρχετο | ἐρχόμενος (A+ ἦν ) | אתה הוה |
| | | | Hebrew |
| 8:5 | διενοούμην | ἤμην συνίων | הייתי מבין |
| 10:2 | ἤμην πενθῶν | | הייתי מתאבל |

| | Hebrew | Greek |
|---|---|---|
| Gen. 4:17 | ויהי בנה | ἦν οἰκοδομῶν |
| 14:12 | הוא ישב | ἦν κατοικῶν |
| 37:2 | היה...רעה | ἦν ποιμαίνων |
| 39:23 | אין...ראה | οὐκ ἦν γινώσκων |
| 40:13 | היית משקהו | ἦσθα οἰνοχοῶν |
| 42:6 | יוסף הוא השליט | ἦν ἄρχων τῆς γῆς |
| I Kngd. 2:11 | היה משרת | ἦν λειτουργῶν |
| 18 | " " | " " |
| 3:1 | " " | " " |
| 7:10 | ויהי מעלה | ἦν ἀναφέρων |
| 14:26 | אין משיג | οὐκ ἦν ἀναστρέφων |

17:34   רעה היה עבדך   ποιμαίνων ἦν ὁ δοῦλος
18:9    ויהי שאול עוין   καὶ ἦν Σαοὺλ ὑποβλεπόμενος
23:26   ויהי נחפז    ἦν σκεπαζόμενος¹

Examples of the treatment of the participle only:

| Hebrew | | LXX | Theodotion |
|---|---|---|---|
| Dan. 4:10 | אמר | ἐφώνησαν | ἐφώνησαν |
| | נחת | ἀπεστάλη | κατέβη |
| 7:5 | אמרין | εἶπεν | ἔλεγον |

The use of the analytic imperfect is found in Josephus:

B.J. I.31.1 καὶ τοῦτο ἦν μάλιστα τάρασσον Ἀντίπατρον

Ant. II.6.7 τί παρόντες εἴημεν;

And in the following paraphrase and original composition:

I Esd. 1:49(51) αὐτοὶ δὲ ἐμυκτήρισαν...καὶ...ἦσαν ἐκπαίζοντες τοὺς προφήτας

II Macc. 1:24 ἦν δὲ προσευχὴ τὸν τρόπον ἔχουσα τοῦτον
(ἦν ἔχουσα  for εἶχε - "had")

15:18 ἦν γὰρ ὁ (φόβος) περὶ γυναικῶν...ἐν ἥττονι μέρει κείμενος αὐτοῖς
("...anxiety for wives weighed less than...")

10:6 μνημονεύοντες ὡς πρὸ μικροῦ χρόνου τὴν τῶν σκηνῶν ἑορτὴν ἐν τοῖς ὄρεσιν καὶ ἐν τοῖς σπηλαίοις θηρίων τρόπον ἦσαν νεμόμενοι

"...remembering that they had been wandering in the mountains and caves like wild beasts..." rather than "...that they had been in the mountains and caves, wandering like wild beasts" i.e. the sphere of the wandering seems to be larger than just caves and mountains.

And in:

III Macc. 3:3 οἱ δὲ Ἰουδαῖοι τὴν μὲν πρὸς τοὺς βασιλεῖς εὔνοιαν ἦσαν φυλάσσοντες    "...continued to maintain..."

---

¹In addition to these the list of analytic imperfects given by Conybeare and Stock (Sel. from LXX 69) was examined, with the result that each example was found to correspond, word for word, to the Hebrew (apart, of course, from those of Susanna, I Maccabees and Baruch).

IV Macc. 4:22 ἐπειδὴ γὰρ πολεμῶν ἦν...ἤκουσέν τε ὅτι κτλ.
(17:6 εἰ δὲ ἔξον ἡμῖν ἦν )

Observations and conclusions:

The periphrastic imperfect is recognized by Moulton (I, 226f) to be a secondary Semitism in the Synoptics. It is permissible Greek; frequency of occurrence is the point at issue. Examples are found throughout the LXX; usually they are not so numerous as to constitute a departure from the practice of the koine (we are leaving out of account the examples from Josephus, II, III, and IV Maccabees, and I Esdras; these merely attest to the presence of the periphrastic imperfect in the koine but tell us nothing about the frequency of its use). Theodotion's version of Daniel--otherwise regarded as extremely literal--uses an analytic 4 out of a possible 28 times. The LXX of Daniel with 15 equivalents for such an imperfect has but one that is periphrastic. The book of I Kingdoms (one third longer than Mark) has ten cases where an analytic is used for a regularly conjugated imperfect. As far as can be determined, every Hebrew analytic tense in this book has a Greek analytic opposite it. There is apparently no reluctance to employ such a form; Greek of the standard and character found in I Kingdoms permits a frequency that is comparatively high (0.3 per page, approximately). In other words, it is "overworked" due to translation, but that overworking is not felt to be inconsistent with the kind of Greek found in that book.

Frequency of occurrence is not characteristic of the koine and is disapproved in a piece of "literary" Greek such as the LXX of Daniel. Although Luke may reject this locution "in every instance where a Markan parallel allows comparison" (Howard, 452), the relative frequency is slightly higher for Luke than for Mark (0.44 per page of the Souter text for Luke, and 0.42 per page for Mark). Matthew is almost completely consistent in correcting Mark's periphrases for the imperfect and in avoiding the use himself.

Thus, (1) Good koine Greek even in translation rejects the usage.

(2) Indifferent Greek permits its appearance.
What we have in Mark may thus be due to translation or, when we take the general character of his Greek into account, we may suppose that it was regarded as unobjectionable. The hypothesis of translation would depend upon this and other secondary Semitisms in a given passage. The analytic imperfect is one of those items of syntax which would help to make a passage "suspect" of being a translation.

17. The use of εἰ negandi (I.9.C.2)

The use of εἰ negandi is conceded by Howard to be a Hebraism (ibid. 468f). Lagrange says (S.Marc lxxxi): "Aramaic has nothing like it, except in the Targums. Probably a reminiscence of the LXX..." Conybeare and Stock show rather conclusively (op. cit. 90) that εἰ is used to render אם where, due to suppression of the apodosis, the former assumes negative force, and that ὅτι is used for affirmative asseverations (sometimes, however, the ὅτι is missing):

I Kngd. 29:6 ζῇ Κύριος ὅτι εὐθὴς σὺ καὶ ἀγαθὸς ἐν ὀφθαλμοῖς μου     (ὅτι translates אם)

III Kngd. 18:15 ζῇ Κύριος...ὅτι σήμερον ὀφθήσομαί σοι
(ὅτι translates כי)

No conjunction–

I Kngd. 1:26 ζῇ ἡ ψυχή σου, ἐγὼ ἡ γυνὴ κτλ.
(no conjunction in Hebrew)

εἰ –

Ps. 94:11 ὡς ὤμοσα ἐν τῇ ὀργῇ μου, Εἰ ἐλεύσονται εἰς τὴν κατάπαυσίν μου        εἰ translates אם

All the following passages have εἰ with negative force as the equivalent of אם : Gen. 14:23; Num. 32:10; Dt. 1:34, 35; I Kngd. 3:14, 14:45, 17:55, 19:6, 28:10; II Kngd. 19:35(36); III Kngd. 2:8;

17:1, 12; 18:10; IV Kngd. 2:2; Ps. 131:3, 4.

The jurative use of εἰ in Mark 8:12 undoubtedly acquires its negative force from its use in the LXX, and it may be set down as a biblicism.

18. Pleonastic ἄρχομαι (I.9.C.4.a.2)

The use of ἄρχομαι with an infinitive where the two are equal to nothing more than the finite form of the verb with which the former appears has been called a "specifically Markan feature"(page 53). Hunkin (op. cit. 391) has made a study of Dalman's citations of the use of the Aramaic שרי and the Mishnaic Hebrew התחיל : he is of the opinion that of the three instances advanced by Dalman as illustrating the use of a meaningless participle שרי not one can be regarded as pleonastic(p. 396); and that possibly 3 of the 5 examples of the use of התחיל parallel the usage of Mark's gospel.

Dalman refers to the abnormal frequency of ἄρχομαι with the infinitive in Enoch 85-90 (Words of Jesus, p. 27): only eight verses of this portion of the book are extant in Greek and in these eight verses ἄρχομαι plus the infinitive occurs 3 times, and a translation of the Ethiopic (in the other part of chs. 85-90) yields " begin" (probably representing ἄρχομαι ) with an infinitive 27 times more. It is difficult to determine how many of these are pleonastic; in many cases they are apparently periphrases for such an expression[1] as "(here and there) dogs were devouring the sheep," 89:42; and there is one case definitely pleonastic: 89:73 "and they began to place a table before the tower." By very arbitrary standards, 1 of these 30 instances is pleonastic; 21, with plural subjects, may be loose periphrases for "here and there" or "one by one"; and in 8 cases "began" is properly used. The

---

[1] 85:10 reads: "And they began to beget many white bulls...one following the other (even) many."

concentration of the word "began" in the section 85-90 is not paralleled in other divisions of the book. In the section 6-36, conceded by Charles (Apoc. & Pseud. II, 172) to have an Aramaic original, "began" appears twice in a narrative not unlike that of 85-90:

> 7:1 "And all the others together with them took unto themselves and each chose for himself one, and they began to go in unto them."
>
> 5 "And they began to sin against birds, and beasts, and reptiles."

Admittedly, this section deals with beginnings; nonetheless, this impression of looseness in the use of "begin" is the same as that made by 85-90. "Begin" is used but three times in the rest of the book:

> 54:2 "And they brought the kings and the mighty and began to cast them into the valley" ( a short interlude of narrative)
>
> 56:7 "And they (the kings) shall begin to fight among themselves"
>
> 61:4 "The elect shall begin to dwell with the elect..."

The "began" of 54:2 is not necessarily pleonastic, although it seems to be the same loose periphrasis found so frequently in the section 85-90; the "begin" of 56:7 and 61:4 is probably rightly used.

Thackeray, who has made a study of the use of ἄρχομαι with an infinitive in Josephus (JTS xxx [1929] 361-70), finds that the first thirteen books of the Antiquities are written in a cruder style than the remaining seven and that one of the marks distinguishing the two sections is the use of pleonastic ἄρχομαι. In his opinion the profusion of this word is due to the "overworking of a form of expression, correct but unusual in good Greek, because it happened to correspond to a phrase that was frequent in the Semitic language" (ibid. 370).

A survey of the occurrences of ἄρχομαι in the LXX yields the following:

Some form of ἄρχομαι translates the hiphil of חלל in 39 cases, 26 of which have "begin" properly used and 13 of which have an idiomatic use. Twice the hiphil of יאל is rendered: once, a distinct "began," and once, an idiomatic "began."

In II Esdras 5:2 שׂריו is translated by ἤρξατο - a distinct "began." IV Maccabees 5:15 has ἤρξατο δημηγορεῖν οὕτως (no interruption). Genesis 2:3 has ἤρξατο ὁ θεὸς ποιῆσαι standing opposite ברא. Exodus 4:10 renders the Hebrew מאז דברך אל־עבדך by ἀφ' οὗ ἤρξω λαλεῖν τῷ θεράποντί σου.

There are two occurrences of a colloquial use of ἄρχομαι in the B Codex where the Masoretic text does not contain the verse in question:

III Kngd. 3:1 Σαλωμῶν ἤρξατο ἀνοίγειν τὰ δυναστεύμ κτλ.

II Chr. 36:4 τότε ἤρξατο ἡ γῆ φορολογεῖσθαι

A great number of examples are found in the books of I Esdras, Tobit, and I Maccabees: there are 8 cases in 448 verses of I Esdras or 1 for every 56 verses; the proportion in Tobit is 1:30; for I Maccabees, 1:103. (The proportion in Mark is 1:25.) The passages from I Esdras are (the distinct and idiomatic cases are listed separately):

2:30 ἤρξαντο κωλύειν τοὺς οἰκοδομοῦντας

3:17 ἤρξατο ὁ πρῶτος...καὶ ἔφη οὕτως

4:1 καὶ ἤρξατο ὁ δεύτερος λαλεῖν

13 ὁ δὲ τρίτος...ἤρξατο λαλεῖν

33 ἤρξατο λαλεῖν περὶ τῆς ἀληθείας

The passages where the meaning is distinctly "began" are:

5:53 ἤρξαντο προσφέρειν θυσίας τῷ θεῷ

56 ἤρξατο Ζοροβαβέλ

6:2 ἤρξαντο οἰκοδομεῖν

Passages from I Maccabees are:

5:2 ἤρξαντο τοῦ θανατοῦν ἐν τῷ λαῷ

9:67 ἤρξαντο τύπτειν

15:40 ἤρξατο τοῦ ἐρεθίζειν τὸν λαόν

And the distinctly "began" passages are:

3:25 ἤρξατο ὁ φόβος Ἰούδα καὶ τῶν ἀδελφῶν

5:31 εἶδεν Ἰούδας ὅτι ἦρκται ὁ πόλεμος

9:73 ἤρξατο Ἰωνάθαν κρίνειν τὸν λαόν

10:10 ἤρξατο οἰκοδομεῖν καὶ καινίζειν τὴν πόλιν

11:46 ἤρξαντο πολεμεῖν

13:42 ἤρξατο ὁ λαὸς Ἰσραὴλ γράφειν

There are two recensions of the book of Tobit: $R^S$ the Sinaitic,[1] and $R^V$ (A, B, al). The relevant passages from this book are as follows:

2:13 ὅτε δὲ ἦλθεν (Ἄννα) πρὸς μέ, ἤρξατο κράζειν

3:1 καὶ περίλυπος γενόμενος τῇ ψυχῇ...ἠρξάμην προσεύχεσθαι ($R^V$ has προσευξάμην)(No interruption until prayer is ended.)

8:5 ἤρξατο Τωβίας λέγειν(from here on only $R^S$ has the text) προσεύχεσθαι καὶ δεηθῆναι ὅπως γένηται αὐτοῖς σωτηρία, καὶ ἤρξατο λέγειν          (No interruption)

19 καὶ ἤρξαντο παρασκευάζειν          (-$R^V$)

10:3 καὶ ἤρξατο λυπεῖσθαι ($R^V$ ἐλυπεῖτο λίαν )

4 καὶ ἤρξατο θρηνεῖν αὐτὸν καὶ εἶπεν

And one passage where the meaning is distinctly "began"-

7:15 καὶ ἤρξαντο ἐσθίειν

Observations-

1. It is passable, though unusual, Greek, as shown by the examples from Xenophon cited on pages 51 and 52.

2. Of the examples adduced by Dalman as illustrating the meaningless use of שרי none is pleonastic. It is used colloquially, however.

3. ἄρχομαι with the infinitive owes its repeated occurrence in the Antiquities of Josephus to the author's familiarity with the Arama-

[1] "the Sinaitic recension, the nearest approach which can be made to the original text whether the latter first appeared in Greek or in a Semitic language"(Simpson, Apoc. and Pseud. I, 175).

ic idiom, so Thackeray thinks.

4. 13 of the 39 examples in the LXX where some form of ἄρχομαι translates the hiphil of חלל have an idiomatic use of "begin"; of two examples of translation equivalents for the hiphil of יאל one has an idiomatic use ("began" appears with "declare").

5. The ἤρξατο of Gen. 2:3, although translating no Hebrew word, represents, as does Exod. 4:10, an attempt to give an exact rendering of the original.

6. The existence of an ἤρξατο in the reading of B for III Kngd. 3:1 and II Chr. 26:4 would point to an independent status for the expression only if the text of the Hebrew, and that text with a "began," were available.

7. The passage from IV Maccabees (composed in Greek) has a colloquial ἄρχομαι with a verb of speaking.

8. Of the passages from I Esdras, 5 have a colloquial use of "began" and 3 a distinct "began." Four of the five are found in chapters 3 and 4, for which, with verses 1-6 from chapter 5, an Aramaic original is posited by Torrey (<u>Ezra</u> <u>Studies</u>, 20-25).

9. The fact that the $R^V$ text of Tobit sees fit to better the Sinaitic ($R^S$) is an action "reflecting a consciousness of their non-Greek character" (Simpson, op.cit. I, 181). Probability supports the view that the book of Tobit originated in the eastern Diaspora and "the original language was certainly Semitic" (Eissfeldt, <u>Einleitung</u>, 724f). As for the Sinaitic recension, there are "Greek sentences and verbal combinations such as could not result at least from literal translation" (Simpson, op. cit. 181); further, as Nöldeke contends (cited by Simpson, <u>ibid</u>. 181), there is a "considerable difference between the Greek style of our book and that of the translations of Judith and I Maccabees."

10. The use of pleonastic ἄρχομαι in I Maccabees is undoubtedly

due to translation, not from Aramaic but from Hebrew.

Conclusions-

The conclusions may be set down in the following manner:

1. Aramaism is a satisfactory explanation of the facts stated in observations 2, 3, 7, 8, 9, and 10.

2. Hebraism is satisfactory for 1, 2, 3,[1] 7, 8,[2] 9, and 10.

3. Secondary Semitism (possible Greek, but "overworked" because of adherence to a Semitic original) is satisfactory for 1, 3, 4, 8, 9, and 10.

The facts of observations 5 and 6 may be set aside as neutral.

The usage in IV Maccabees may be a Semitism of thought not due to translation or it may be an instance of colloquial usage (Greek).

It will be seen that translation making frequent use of a possible colloquial Greek construction is one origin for the locution and that Aramaism or Hebraism of thought not due to translation are nearly equally acceptable for the others. From observation 2 there have been adduced examples not of a meaningless, but of a colloquial, use of "begin," and from observation 4, that the locution owes its frequency to the Hebrew is a matter of direct observation.

In the latter half of the books of Acts we have what is almost surely a Semitism in a pleonastic use of ἄρχομαι :

18:26 οὗτός τε ἤρξατο παρρησιάζεσθαι ἐν τῇ συναγωγῇ

24:2 ἤρξατο κατηγορεῖν ὁ Τέρτυλλος

27:35 καὶ κλάσας ἤρξατο ἐσθίειν

Pleonastic ἄρχομαι may have more than one status. Where it oc-

---

[1]This usage may be something other than an Aramaism--and Thackeray notes the possibility.
[2]Howard (op.cit. 455) says:"This (pleonastic ἄρχομαι ) cannot be called a Hebraism, for though it is found fairly often in the LXX, a glance at Hatch-Redpath shows it has no fixed original. Observation 4 shows the hiphil of חלל is almost exclusively responsible for the use of ἄρχομαι in the LXX either idiomatically or as a real "began."

curs in translation it is to be viewed as a secondary Semitism; where in free composition, it may be a Semitism of thought. As a secondary Semitism the locution may in Mark be the product of translation from an Aramaic source, although the possibility of a Hebrew original is not to be disallowed.[1] The possibility of its belonging to the colloquial usages of the koine must be admitted as well; the frequency in Mark may be due to his non-literary style.

### 19. The redundant use of ἀναστάς, ἀφείς, and ἐλθών (I.9.C.5.a)

Lagrange points out (op. cit.lxxxvii) that there is no need of seeing an Aramaic idiom in the use of the participle ἀφείς in Mark 4:36 and 8:13, and that the participle ἀναστάς in 1:35 and 2:14 is not redundant. These participles may be redundant where they occur with a verb of motion or a verb of departure: ἀφέντες ἀπῆλθον (12:12), ἀφέντες ἔφυγον (14:50), ἀναστὰς ἀπῆλθεν (7:24), ἐκεῖθεν ἀναστὰς ἔρχεται (10:1). The coupling of the verb ἀνιστάναι in participial or finite form with a verb of motion or departure is common in the LXX:

| Gen 13:17 | קום התהלך | ἀναστὰς διόδευσον |
| 19:14 | קומו צאו | ἀνάστητε καὶ ἐξέλθατε |
| 15 | קום קח | ἀναστὰς λαβέ |
| 21:18 | קומי שאי | ἀνάστηθι καὶ λαβέ |

Cf. 22:3, 19; 24:10; 25:34; 27:43; 28:2; 32:1; 35:1, 3; 28:19; 43:8, 13, 15; 44:4.

A coördinate construction of the type of Gen. 4:8 is found in the following passages: 21:14, 32; 23:3, 7; 28:18; 37:7; 46:5 (in the original there are intervening words in every case:

---

[1] J.M. Grintz contends (JBL lxxix [1960] 32-47) that Hebrew was a living language in the closing days of the Second Temple.

Gen. 4:8 καὶ ἐγένετο ἐν τῷ εἶναι αὐτοὺς ἐν τῷ πεδίῳ καὶ ἀνέστη Κάιν ἐπὶ Ἄβελ τὸν ἀδελφὸν αὐτοῦ καὶ ἀπέκτεινεν αὐτόν

And for Exodus:

| Coördinate construction | Participle |
|---|---|
| 1:8; 12:31 (two imperatives); 32:1 (two imperatives) | 2:7; 24:13 (with several words intervening) |

For Numbers:

| | |
|---|---|
| 16:25 (one word intervening) | 11:32 (several words intervening) |
| 23:18 (two imperatives) | 22:13  "      "       " |
| | 14      "      "       " |
| | 20      "      "       " |
| | 21      "      "       " |
| | 24:25   "      "       " |

For Deuteronomy:

| | |
|---|---|
| 18:18 (several words intervening) | 17:8 |
| | 31:16 |

In I Esdras:

4:47 τότε ἀναστὰς Δ. ὁ βασιλεῦς κατεφίλησεν αὐτόν

8:95 ἀναστὰς ἐπιτέλει

96 ἀναστὰς Ἐ. ὤρκισεν

9:1 ἀναστὰς Ἐ. ἐπορεύθη

7 ἀναστὰς Ἐ. εἶπεν

Observations:

1. In Genesis there are 16 examples of the second aorist participle of ἀνιστάναι used with a verbum finitum. A participle and an imperative stand opposite two Hebrew imperatives in asyndeton in 7 cases; and opposite two coördinate Hebrew verbs in 9 cases. In one case (32:1) a participle appears representing a verb separated from the coördinate verb by several words.

2. In Numbers the participle with the finite verb appears in a number of cases where several words intervene in the original between the coördinate verbs.

3. The participle, in Genesis at least, tends to be used where one

coordinate verb immediately follows the other in the Hebrew. Intervening words may reasonably be thought to account for the use of a coördinate construction in the Greek in 7 cases (4:8; 21:14; 23:3, 7; 28:18; 37:7; 46:5)(this distinction in use of the participle with a finite verb as against a coördinate construction does not obtain in the remainder of the Pentateuch); coordinate constructions in 19:14 and 21:18 render asyndetic couplings of Hebrew imperatives, however.

4. The participle-finite verb rendering is found in the four books of Kingdoms three or four times: II Kngd. 15:9; 17:7(8); III Kngd. 14:12; IV Kngd. 1:3 (A- στηθι καί ); the majority of renderings has a coördinate construction.

5. The combination of ἀνίστημι with a verb of motion is not found in the Greek equivalent to the Aramaic section of Daniel; pleonastic קום does not occur in the Aramaic portions of Daniel and Ezra.

Before conclusions are formulated regarding the use of the participle ἀναστάς let us turn to the reasons for the appearance of the participle ἐλθών. Just how redundant the participle is in the examples in Mark is problematical. "...come (came) and..." seems little more than a colloquial expression in 5:23, 7:25, and 12:42. In 16:1 ἵνα ἐλθοῦσαι ἀλείψωσιν αὐτόν, ἐλθοῦσαι seems more superfluous than in the three instances just mentioned. And in the καὶ ἐλθὼν εὐθὺς προσελθών of 14:45 the repetition serves to emphasize the directness with which Judas executed the act of betrayal.

The following passages in Genesis have a participle and finite verb translating a Hebrew paratactic construction; it is to be observed that all the examples of ἐλθών are used with a verb other than that of going:[1]

---

[1] Lagrange observes (op.cit. lxxxvii) that, while the figure is Hebraic as well as Aramaic, the correspondence with Aramaic is more nearly complete since that language never employs two consecutive verbs in the sense of 'going.'

| 13:18 | ויבא...וישב | ἐλθών...κατῴκησε |
| 24:42 | ויבא...ויאמר | καὶ ἐλθών...εἶπα |
| 27:35 | בא...ויקח | ἐλθών...ἔλαβεν |
| 32:11(12) | ויבא...והכני | ἐλθών...πατάξῃ |
| 47:1 | ויבא...ויגד | ἐλθών...ἀπήγγειλεν |
| 50:18 | וילכו...ויפלו לפניו ויאמרו | ἐλθόντες πρὸς αὐτὸν εἶπαν |

Examples from Exodus are:

| 2:8 | ותלך...תקרא | ἐλθοῦσα ἐκάλεσε |
| 15 | וישב | ἐλθὼν ἐκάθισεν |
| 3:16 | לך ואספת | ἐλθὼν συνάγαγε |
| 8:25(21) | לכו זבחו | ἐλθόντες θύσατε |
| 35:10 | ויבאו ויעשו | ἐλθὼν ἐργαζέσθω |

In the section II Kngd. 11:3- III Kngd. 2:11, which Thackeray says (op.cit. 13) is one of the parts of the LXX that are characterized by "literal or unintelligent versions," we find the following treatment of Hebrew parataxis:

| 11:22 | ויבא יגד לדוד | παρεγένετο καὶ ἀπήγγειλεν |
| 12:1 | ויבא...ויאמר | εἰσῆλθεν...καὶ εἶπεν |
| 20 | ויבא...ישתחו | " ... " προσεκύνησεν |
| 24 | ויבא...וישכב | " ... " ἐκοιμήθη |
| 13:24 | ויבא...ויאמר | ἦλθεν...καὶ εἶπεν |
| 14:31 | ויבא...ויאמר | " ... " " |
| 33 | ויבא...ויגד | εἰσῆλθεν...καὶ ἀπήγγειλεν |
| 33 | ויבא...וישתחו | " ... " προσεκύνησεν |
| 19:6 | ויבא...ויאמר | " ... " εἶπεν |
| 20:3 | ויבא...ויקח | " ... " ἔλαβεν |
| 24:13 | ויבא...ויגד | " ... " ἀνήγγειλεν |
| 18 | ויבא...ויאמר | " ... " εἶπεν |
| III Kngd. 1:23 | ויבא...ישתחו | " ... " προσεκύνησεν |

53

The participle ἐλθών does not occur in this section.

The construction (ἐλθών with a verbum finitum) is much less frequent in the last three books of the Pentateuch (it is found but once: Dt. 17:3); it seems as though the translator(s) gradually abandoned the attempt to render into idiomatic Greek the repeated occurrence of a verb for "go" coördinate with another verb. But it must be noted that the proportion of verbs for "come" and "go" is considerably higher in Genesis than in any other book of the Pentateuch. In the historical books, exclusive of the Pentateuch, (ending with II Chronicles), the participle (2nd aorist or present) of ἔρχεσθαι unaccompanied by the article, is found but three or four times. ἐλθών with a finite verb occurs in II Maccabees 2:5; III Macc. 2:10; Tobit 2:3; ἐρχόμενος in II Macc. 8:6.

Observations:

1. The coupling of a participle of ἔρχεσθαι (chiefly the second aorist) and a finite verb occurs with greatest frequency in the Pentateuch and more particularly in Genesis; that participle renders a Hebrew finite verb which is in a coördinate relation with another finite verb.[1]

2. In 15 examples, taken from a section designated as of the "literal" or "unintelligent" sections of the LXX, the Hebrew coördinate verbs are rendered by coördinate constructions in the Greek.[2]

3. The construction is seldom found in books of the LXX other than those of the Pentateuch: it occurs twice in II Maccabees where (as well as III Maccabees) its presence cannot be attributed to translation.

Conclusions:

---

[1] The coördinate construction is found in the Greek of Genesis 20:3; 24:32; 26:17; 27:30; 28:9; 29:30; 31:20; 47:1.
[2] 17 examples of a coördinate construction are found in I Kingdoms, termed "indifferent Greek" by Thackeray.

The somewhat redundant use of the participles ἀναστάς and ἐλθών is the result of rendering Hebrew asyndetic and paratactic constructions, but uniform occurrence of this use is not found in the historical sections of the LXX: apparently the Greek begins to adhere more closely to the parataxis of the Hebrew in the course of translating the several books. If any inference from the treatment of the Hebrew by the Greek is possible, it is that in rendering two coördinate Hebrew verbs only the coupling of participle and finite verb was held to be consistent with koine practice; such coupling is greatest in Genesis and diminishes toward the end of the historical books. Concerning the fact that these participles are found in such books as II and III Maccabees, and ἀναστάς in I Esdras, we may say this: koine Greek may have been influenced by Hebrew or Aramaic to the extent of incorporating these slightly redundant participles.

The participle ἀφείς with a verb of motion or departure does not occur in the LXX. It must be remembered that we stated (page 55, note 3) that the use of ἀφείς was not so clearly redundant in Mark. Dalman furnishes us with examples from Jewish Aramaic of the coupling of two verbs of departure (Worte Jesu 17):

j. Sabb. 8 c    שבקיה ואזל ליה    "he left him and went on"
j. Taan. 66 c   שבקוניה ואזלון לון   "they left him and went away"

These indicate that the use of a superfluous verb of departure has an Aramaic source; analogy with ἐλθών would suggest that koine usage is responsible for the dropping of the paratactic construction in the Greek in favor of the participle-finite verb combination. There is at hand no control passages whereby to test a supposition of translation as accounting for the possibly redundant participles of ἀφίημι found in Mark 12:12 and 14:50.

20. The use of the participle ἀποκριθείς (I.9.C.5.a)

The participle ἀποκριθείς in the LXX stands opposite the Hebrew expressions found in the following passages:

| Gen. | | | |
|---|---|---|---|
| 18:9 | ויאמר - | ἀποκριθεὶς εἶπεν | |
| 27 | ויען ויאמר | " | " |
| 23:10 | ויען לאמר | " | " |
| | (cf. 14 ἀπεκρίθη for ויען לאמר) | | |
| 24:50 | ויען לבן ובתואל ויאמרו | ἀποκριθεὶς...εἶπαν | |
| 27:37 | ויען ויאמר | ἀποκριθεὶς εἶπεν | |
| 31:14 | ותען...ותאמרנה | ἀποκριθεῖσαι Ῥ.καὶ Λ. εἶπαν | |
| 31 | ויען ויאמר | ἀποκριθεὶς εἶπε | |
| 36 | ויען ויאמר | " | " |
| 43 | ויען ויאמר | " | " |
| 40:18 | ויען ויאמר | " | " |
| 41:16 | ויען לאמר | " | " |
| 42:22 | ויען לאמר | " | " |

The following passages have the coördinate type of construction, ἀπεκρίθη καὶ εἶπεν rendering the Hebrew type ויען ויאמר: I Kngd. 1:15, 17; 4:17; 9:12, 19, 21; 10:12; 14:12, 28; 16:18; 21:4(5), 5(6); 22:14; 23:4; 25:10; 26:6, 22; 30:2. In 22:9 ἀποκρίνεται replaces ἀπεκρίθη. ἀπεκρίθη καὶ εἶπεν translates ויען in 20:28; εἶπεν, ויען ויאמר in 26:14; and ἀπεκρίθη, ויען ויאמר in 29:9. The participle does not occur in I Kingdoms.

Greek equivalents for this usage in the Aramaic section of Daniel are:

| | Aramaic | LXX | Theodotion |
|---|---|---|---|
| 2:5 | ענה ואמר | ἀποκριθεὶς δὲ εἶπε | ἀπεκρίθη |
| 7 | ענו ואמרין | ἀπεκρίθησαν δὲ λέγοντες | ἀπεκρίθησαν...καὶ εἶπαν |
| 8 | ענה ואמר | καὶ εἶπεν | καὶ ἀπεκρίθη...καὶ εἶπεν |

| | | | |
|---|---|---|---|
| 10 | ענו ואמרן | καὶ ἀπεκρίθησαν- | καὶ ἀπεκρίθησαν... καὶ λέγουσιν |
| 26 | ענה ואמר | ἀποκριθεὶς δὲ εἶπε- | καὶ ἀπεκρίθη... καὶ εἶπε |
| 27 | ענה ואמר | εἶπεν ἐκφωνήσας- | καὶ ἀπεκρίθη... καὶ λέγει |
| 47 | ענה ואמר | εἶπεν- | καὶ ἀποκριθεὶς...εἶπεν. |
| 3:14 | ענה ואמר | εἶπεν (συνιδών)- | καὶ ἀπεκρίθη... καὶ εἶπεν |
| 16 | ענו ואמרין | ἀποκριθέντες εἶπαν- | καὶ ἀπεκρίθησαν ...λέγοντες |
| 28(95) | ענה ואמר | ὑπολαβών...εἶπεν- | καὶ ἀπεκρίθη... καὶ εἶπεν |
| 4:16 | ענה ואמר | ἀπεκρίθη- | καὶ ἀπεκρίθη...καὶ εἶπεν |
| 27 | ענה ואמר | ἀποκριθεὶς εἶπεν- | καὶ " " " |
| 5:10 | ענה ואמרת | (Paraphrase) | εἶπεν |
| 13 | ענה ואמר | ἀποκριθεὶς εἶπεν- | εἶπεν |
| 17 | ענה ואמר | ἀπεκρίθη- | " |
| 6:12(13) | ענה ואמר | ἀποκριθεὶς εἶπεν- | " |
| 13(14) | ענו ואמרין | εἶπον- | ἀπεκρίθησαν καὶ λέγουσιν |
| 7:16 | ואמר | ἀποκριθεὶς λέγει- | εἶπεν |

The Sinaitic recension of Tobit has the participle-finite verb coupling in 6 instances as against $R^V$'s 2; Judith (6:17) and Esther (7:3) each have it once- in fact, the only passages in the LXX other than those already designated which contain ἀποκρίνεσθαι in a participial form are Joshua 1:16; 24:16; Job 1:7; Isaiah 3:7; 21:19; I Maccabees 15:33; and II Maccabees 7:8 ὁ δὲ ἀποκριθεὶς προσεῖπεν 15:14 has the participle with an infinitive ἀποκριθέντα τὸν ὄντα εἰπεῖν.

Observations:

1. ἀποκριθεὶς εἶπεν translates in Genesis ויאמר, לאמר ויען and ויען ויאמר.

2. There is little correspondence between the reading of the LXX and that of the Aramaic for Daniel: participle and verbum finitum (ἀποκριθεὶς...εἶπε[λέγει])or simply ἀπεκρίθη are preferred. Where no reply is called for (2:27; 3:14, 28; 5:13) the LXX has ἐκφωνήσας, συνιδών and ὑπολαβών (5:13 is an exception in that the Greek, as well as the Aramaic, has a word for reply where there is no question of a reply).

3. Theodotion in translating the Aramaic section of Daniel has 10 coördinate constructions where a form of ἀποκρίνεσθαι occurs: 1 with the participle of this verb and the finite form of a verb of saying; 1 with the finite form of ἀποκρίνεσθαι and the participle of a verb of saying; in 1 case he has ἀπεκρίθη translating the Aramaic coördinate participles ענה ואמר ; in 5 cases εἶπεν renders a coördinate construction of either finite verbs or participles in the Aramaic.

4. The fact that ἀποκριθεὶς (προσ)εῖπεν is found in II Maccabees would indicate that the locution was present in the koine.

Conclusions:

The fact that ἀποκριθεὶς εἶπεν(λέγει)translates (observation 1) the Hebrew locutions ויאמר, ויען לאמר, ויען ויאמר and the Aramaic ענה ואמר and ואמר (LXX of Dan. 7:16) indicates that it is a fixed phrase,[1] modelled on a Semitic usage but not depending on a Semitic original for its form in every instance where it is used to translate. The lack of correspondence between the LXX and the Aramaic of Daniel (observation 2), with the Greek employing four or five dif-

---

[1] In Aramaic "answered and said" occurs sometimes when nobody has said anything. If ἀποκριθεὶς εἶπεν is a fixed phrase it may similarly occur in a free Greek composition where there is no question of a reply.

ferent ways to render the practically unvaried phrase in the original, ranges alongside the fixed phrase explanation: ἀποκριθεὶς εἶπεν ·(λέγει) is apparently but one type selected to translate the Aramaic. We may infer from the fact that the locution does not appear in such a book as I Kingdoms (designated indifferent Greek by Thackeray) that the translators, tiring of rendering the Hebrew construction into passable Greek, chose to follow the paratactic original; this seems to be the case with ἐλθών and ἀναστάς as well. Thus ἀποκριθεὶς εἶπεν (λέγει) seems at least to have the status of a permissible koine usage; as such a "Semitism of thought" best explains its occurrence in a "free Greek" composition such as II Maccabees (as it also does that of ἐλθών). Its form, originally due to translation, made it a ready vehicle in rendering a Semitic locution. Dalman's statement (Worte Jesu 20), "In later (than biblical) Jewish Aramaic this formula is quite unknown" would apparently rule out the necessity of supposing translation to account for its presence in Mark.

21. The use of the phrase ἐν ἐκείναις ταῖς ἡμέραις
(I.11.A)

The phrase ἐν ἐκείναις ταῖς ἡμέραις translates the Hebrew words בימים ההם (ἐν ἐκείνῃ τῇ ἡμέρᾳ- ביום ההוא) passim. In the following passages where the Greek phrase occurs there are no equivalent Hebrew words: Dt. 17:12; 31:10 (singular); 32:44; Jos. 9:12 (sing.), 24:33 (sing.); I Kngd. 4:1, 14:45 (sing); I Chr. 10:6 (sing.) Isa. 30:25 (sing.); Dan. (LXX) 5:1. It is also found in III Macc. 7:15 (sing.).[1] In the New Testament, exclusive of the Gospels, Acts and Revelation, it is found in II Thess. 1:10 (sing.); II Tim. 1:12 (acc. sing. with εἰς), 18 (sing.), 4:8 (sing.); in all these passages the

---

[1] The phrase ἀπ' ἐκείνων τῶν καιρῶν occurs in II Maccabees 15:37.

singular form of the expression seems to be a stereotyped term having an eschatological reference. The plural in the "little apocalypse" of Mark 13 (verses 17, 19, 24, 32) and the singular in the words at the Last Supper (14:25) have a future and eschatological reference; the singular in 2:20 is also future though not so definitely eschatological. A general time designation (past) is all that is conveyed by the plural form of 1:9 and 8:1; a specific designation (past) is the singular of 4:35--this is also the case with the singular of III Macc. 7:15. The use of the term for the designations of future time is due to its being a fixed phrase, probably acquired from the LXX. The bulk of the examples in the Greek of the Old Testament used where there are no corresponding words in the Hebrew refer to the past (as they do in Mark 1:9 and 8:1); the plural of Dt. 17:12 is future and non-eschatological; the singular of Isa. 30:25, future and eschatological. Thus, ἐν ἐκείναις ταῖς ἡμέραις is clearly to be classed as a biblicism.

Conclusions

At the beginning of this study the question was asked: Can a place be assigned the Greek of Mark's gospel in the development of the koine? This question was to be answered after two things had been done. First, an inquiry as to the degree and kind of divergence from the Attic standard in the Greek of Mark and that of a body of papyri approximately contemporary with Mark was to be made. Second, there would be an attempt to explain divergences from the Attic standard found in Mark but not paralleled in the papyri. Could these latter usages, although they are not found in the papyri of the period chosen for the study, be said to belong to Hellenistic usage? If they could not, how were we to account for them?

In part I Mark and the papyri were found to agree in a number of variations from the Attic standard. Some 60 instances of outstanding divergence in syntax were considered. In all but 21 of these instances the usage of Mark followed that of the papyri: in some cases the usage had developed early in the Hellenistic period; in others papyri and Mark more or less simultaneously exhibit the same usage. To illustrate the relation between papyri and Mark, we shall make use again of the analogy of intersecting circles which we employed in the statement of the problem. The 60 instances considered may represent the total area in the intersecting circles. In some of these 60 cases of divergence Mark and the papyri agree-- that is the overlapping area. The extent of this area is indicated by the ratio of agreement to disagreement, in divergence, between the two (39:21), although it is of course not simply a matter of numbers. Certain items of the agreement, such as the use of the genitive absolute, that of the dative of specification, and that of ὅτι recitativum, may be more striking or occur more frequently than the others, but in the sum of variations are probably no more important. At all events, we may say that most, if not all, are essential rather than incidental agreements, and that, in the main, the Greek of the papyri and that of Mark are phases of the same development.

The statement just made stands, irrespective of the conclusions at which we may arrive regarding the usages of Mark that are outside the area common to the intersected circles (and inside the Markan circle). However, this fact may be used to support more than one conclusion. If, after considering extensions of Hellenistic usage, we can establish a probability that the usages of Mark which remain unexplained from part I belong to the koine, then no other hypothesis than composition in Greek is needed to explain Mark's Greek. If the unexplained usages may be paralleled in the koine, but the frequency with which they occur arouses a query whether some other explanation than composition in Greek may not more readily account for them, another hypothesis may be advanced, i.e. translation; but the community between Mark and the papyri will remain without modification. Accordingly, the pivot upon which our conclusions turn is the Markan usages unexplained in part I, which we may for convenience call "Markisms."

There are the following possible explanations of these Markan usages, or Markisms:[1]

(1) Hellenistic usage other than that found in the papyri;

(2) usages which upon further examination can be said to agree with those of Attic Greek or with those of the papyri (since they may be said to agree with Attic or the papyri, they are only apparent Markisms);

(3) biblicism;

(4) primary Semitism--awkward Greek due to unfamiliarity with Greek or to the necessity of adhering to a Semitic original;

---

[1] The terms used to explain the Markisms have already been used in the discussion in part II.

(5) secondary Semitism - permissible Greek usage, but overworked due to translation;

(6) tertiary Semitism - i.e. a Semitism of thought not necessarily due to translation (ordinarily called "Hebraism", "Aramaism", or "Semitism").[1]

Clearly, if the unexplained usages may be accounted for by (1), (2), (3), or (6), translation is not a necessary hypothesis. In the case of a relatively high proportion of the usages classified under (5) being found, translation is a probable hypothesis, and a relatively high proportion under (4) will point to this same explanation. But (3) and (6) are of a neutral character: usages that may be biblicisms or Semitisms of thought can be expected in free Greek composition, but the fact that they are unusual Greek makes them susceptible of another explanation: translation from a Semitic original.

The following explanations for each item of Markan usage treated in part II are given in the order of probability; there is no enumeration where one seems as probable as the other:

(a) The use of ἴδε with a nominal sentence - Permissible Attic and koine usage

(b) The third plural impersonal indefinite - Vernacular Greek
Secondary Semitism

(c) The distributive singular -
1. Permissible Attic and koine usage
2. Biblicism

(d) The use of plurals - Biblicism

(e) The nominative in time designations-
1. Primary Semitism
2. Permissible Attic and koine usage

(f) The nominative with the article in place of the vocative
1. Permissible Attic and koine usage
2. Secondary Semitism

---

[1]"Primary," "Secondary," and "Tertiary" are not subdivisions of "Semitisms" exactly; rather, they indicate if anything the degrees of likelihood that a Semitic original is responsible for the reading in the Greek: greatest in the case of a primary, least in the case of a tertiary.

(g) The dative with πιστεύειν ἐν   Primary Semitism

(h) The use of διὰ χειρός   
1. Biblicism
2. Semitism of thought (tertiary Semitism)

(i) The use of ἐπί and the accusative where περί and the genitive would seem to be proper   
1. Coincidence in Greek and Semitic idiom
2. Semitism of thought

(j) The use of the positive degree of the adjective for the comparative   
1. Permissible Attic and koine usage
2. Primary Semitism

(k) The use of a cardinal for an ordinal   Biblicism

(l) Duplication as a distributive designation   Biblicism

(m) The redundant pronoun   Biblicism
Secondary Semitism

(n) Redundant words   Vernacular Greek

(o) The use of οὐ(μὴ)...πᾶς for οὐδείς   
1. Hebraism (Tertiary Semitism)
2. Biblicism

(p) ἔρχεται as equivalent to the passive of φέρειν   Primary Semitism

(q) The analytic imperfect   Vernacular Greek
Secondary Semitism

(r) The use of εἰ negandi   Biblicism

(s) Pleonastic ἄρχομαι   Secondary Semitism
Vernacular Greek
Tertiary Semitism

(t) The redundant use of ἀναστάς and ἐλθών (questionable)   
Tertiary Semitism
Primary Semitism

(u) The redundant use of ἀποκριθείς   Tertiary Semitism

(v) The phrase ἐν ἐκείναις ταῖς ἡμέραις   Biblicism

It will be seen that:

(1) in 3 cases (e), (g), and (p) a primary Semitism points to translation;

(2) in 6 cases (d), (h), (k), (l), (r), and (v) the presence of a biblicism may mean either translation or composition in Greek;

(3) in 5 cases (a), (c), (f), (j), and (n) permissible Greek is

found, necessitating no hypothesis except composition in Greek;

(4) in 4 cases (b), (m), (q), and (s), the possibilities of translation and composition are more or less equal;

(5) in one case (i) a coincidence in idiom is of the same character as a biblicism or Semitism of thought: it may mean either translation or composition in Greek;

(6) in one case (t) the findings are questionable;

(7) in one case there is a Semitism of thought (tertiary Semitism) (u), and in one (o) a Hebraism - both of which, as we noted above, may be placed either on the side of composition or on that of translation.

All of the examples for which translation is the most likely explanation are "sayings" passages (the fact that they are "sayings" passages is itself one reason for supposing translation responsible). Similarly, the instances where translation is listed second in the order of probability,--viz. the nominative with the article in place of the vocative, the positive degree of the adjective in place of the comparative, the personal pronoun used redundantly when there is already a relative pronoun in a clause,[1] εἰ negandi--all occur in "sayings" passages. The locutions whose weight would seem to swing the balance for or against translation for the gospel as a whole are those which occur relatively frequently and that in non-sayings passages: the third plural impersonal, the distributive singular, the use of plurals where an idea in the singular is in mind, the analytic imperfect, pleonastic ἄρχομαι pleonastic ἀποκριθείς and the phrase ἐν ἐκείναις ταῖς ἡμέραις. Three of these (the use of plurals, distributive singular, and ἐν ἐκείναις ταῖς ἡμέραις ) have already been classed as biblicisms; one (pleonastic ἀποκριθείς), as a Semitism of thought not due to trans-

---

[1] Mark 3:31, which contains redundant possessive pronouns, is not a "saying," but the usage was noted as agreeing with the vernacular of the papyri (above, p. 37).

lation; and the remaining three, the third plural impersonal, the analytic imperfect, and pleonastic ἄρχομαι are "overworked", either because of translation or because of the looseness of Mark's non-literary style.

Although translation is not necessary to explain the presence of any one of the usages just mentioned as relatively frequent, cognizance must be taken of the crowding together of these and "neutral" usages in any given passage. Such crowding may point to translation, provided the biblicisms, Semitisms of thought, and secondary Semitisms are all possible Aramaisms. The tabulation which follows includes only non-sayings passages in which Markisms are found:

Chapter 1: 9, 10, 11, 32, 35, 45
2: 3, 6, 14, 18, 23
3: 33
5: 17, 20
6: 2, 7 (bis), 34 (bis), 37, 39, 40, 52, 55
7: 24, 25, 32
8: 1, 11, 22, 29, 32
9: 4, 5, 19, 22
10: 3, 13, 22, 24, 28, 32 (bis), 41, 47, 51
11: 14, 15, 22, 33
12: 1, 12(?), 13, 35, 42
13: 5
14: 4, 45, 48, 54, 65, 69
15: 2, 9, 8, 12, 18
16: 1, 2

The inclusion of sayings passages in this table would increase the number of Markisms in all chapters slightly, and in chapter 13, considerably (10 instead of 1).

Some usages in the area of agreement between Mark and the papyri may have the neutral character that Semitisms of thought or biblicisms do, provided they are possible Aramaic. That is to say, some of the usages treated in part I which agreed with the papyri in diverging from the Attic norm may be capable of a different explanation and may count with the Markisms just tabulated as evidences of translation. If we add these [1] to the tabulation just given we have:

1: 9(bis), 10, 11(bis), 32, 35, 45

2: 3, 6, 14, 18, 23

3: 5, 21, 31, 33

4: 38

5: 6, 17, 20, 22

6: 2, 7(bis), 17, 34(bis), 37, 39, 40, 52, 55

7: 24, 25, 26, 32

8: 1, 3, 11, 22, 29, 32

9: 4, 5, 17, 19, 21, 22

10: 3, 10, 13, 17, 22, 24, 28, 32(bis), 41, 47, 51

11: 13, 14, 15, 22, 33

12: 1, 12(?), 13, 35, 42

13: 3, 5

14: 4, 45, 48, 54(bis), 65, 69

15: 8, 12, 18, 27, 29, 38, 40

16: 1, 2

We may inquire as to the extent of a possible original. Most of the suspect usages occur either within a story or in what is apparently the beginning of a section; instances of the latter are to be regarded as parts of the mise-en-scene of the story or incident, perhaps denoting attendant circumstance, as is the case with the following passages: 1:9,

---

[1] The usages are: the nominal sentence, $ἀπό$ with the gen. in place of the acc., dative of specification, the use of $εἰς$ for $ἐν$, $ἐπί$ and the acc. as equivalent to "where?", $παρά$ and the genitive, $εἰς$ used as an indefinite pronoun, $εἰς$ used as a correlative, repetition of the personal pronoun, pleonastic words, $ὅτι$ introductory, and pleonastic prepositions ( $ὅτι$ recitativum is not tabulated).

32, 35; 2:18, 23; 3:31; 4:1; 6:2, 7, 17, 34; 7:24; 8:11, 17, 22; 10:13, 28, 32; 11:15; 12:13, 35; 13:5. Sentences of a generalizing or summarizing character, which are more likely to be the words of the composer of the gospel than to belong to his sources, are as follows: 1:39; 2:1a; the section 3:7-12; 4:33, 34; 6:6b, 55, 56; 7:31; 8:1; 9:30; 10:1; 12:38. 8:1 may be a designation of attendant circumstances and as such belong to the story of the feeding of the four thousand. Some of the generalizing statements occur at the close of a story, as in the following: 1:45c; 5:20b; 6:5, 6a, 13; 12:17b, 34b, 37b. In addition to these we may select certain "bridge" passages or statements--also to be regarded as the work of the composer rather than as belonging to possible source stories: 5:1; 7:1, 24; 8:27; 10:46.

Among the latter three groups of passages Markisms are found in 7:24 (the ἀναστάς may not be redundant, of course) and 8:1. When it is recalled that 8:1 may denote either attendant circumstances or summary, it would seem that there is no decisive indication that suspect usages are found in passages which may be regarded as the composition of the author of the second gospel. In other words, the "editorial" sentences are not subject to the same degree of suspicion that those which intro- the stories are. But the sentences considered in the groups of summarizing or "bridge" passages are admittedly a very small part of the gospel, and the presence or absence of Markisms in such a limited field would not be very significant.

The presumption is that, if a number of locutions point to a possible Semitic original, that original which is responsible for the "stretch" of suspect usages included the story with its introductory statement and that it was translated intact. Translation as a possible hypothesis would seem to cover at least the stories, severally, and with the less likelihood, the summarizing statements or "bridge" passages.

Summary:

To account for the Greek of the gospel of Mark translation is not a necessary hypothesis; in the case of "sayings" passages translation is of course conceded. All passages which show Semitic influence at work may be examples of forms which have "silted through into the koine" or are a part of the thought forms of one whose mind was stored with the expressions of the Septuagint. However, the crowding of locutions stamped as Semitic in any given "stretch" raises the presumption of translation. The Semitic coloring is uniform enough to give us to suppose that in many cases the whole story with introductory statements was composed in Aramaic and later translated into Greek, the Greek form being the one which came to the hand of the composer of the gospel.

There is nothing within the scope of this study which will enable us to say whether the balance of probability rests with composition in Greek or with translation; the burden of proof would seem to rest with those who advocate the latter, and the methods of proof would seem to be other than those employed in this study.[1]

---

[1] In this concluding section the suggestions regarding a possible Semitic original have been framed keeping in mind some of the considerations set forth by Millar Burrows in an article in the JBL, "Mark's Transitions and the Translation Hypothesis" (xlviii 1929 117). I have made no reference to C.C.Torrey's position regarding Aramaic originals for the whole of each of the gospels. His argument is based largely upon cases of (at least alleged) mistranslation. While mistranslation, in the nature of the case, can rarely if ever be fully demonstrated, a few very probable instances, coupled with the facts just given, might make a very convincing case for translation. To evaluate this argument would be, as I have hinted, to leave the area of my investigation, and such evaluation requires a competence in Semitics to which I make no claim.

BIBLIOGRAPHY


Allen, W.C., The Gospel according to Saint Mark with introduction and
   notes, by Willoughby C. Allen. (The Oxford Church Biblical
   Commentary) London, 1915

Apocrypha and Pseudepigrapha, The Apocrypha and Pseudepigrapha of the
   Old Testament in English. Ed. by R.H.Charles, 2 vols. Oxford
   1913.

Black, M., An Aramaic Approach to the Gospels and Acts, Oxford, 1946

Blass, F., A Grammar of New Testament Greek by Friedrich Blass. Tr. by
   Henry St. John Thackeray. London, 1898.

Brugmann- Thumb, Griechische Grammatik. K. Brugmann. 4 Aufl. bearb.v.
   A. Thumb. München, 1913 (Handbuch der Kl. Altertumswiss. von
   J. von Müller. II Band, Abt. I).

Burney, C.F., The Aramaic Origin of the Fourth Gospel, by C.F.Burney.
   Oxford, 1922.

Classical Quarterly, London, 1907ff.

Conybeare and Stock, Selections from the Septuagint, by F.C.Conybeare
   and St.G. Stock. Boston, 1905.

Dalman, G., Die Worte Jesu, von G. Dalman. Leipzig, 1898.
   The Words of Jesus, by G. Dalman. Eng. ed. tr. by D.M.Kay,
   Edinburgh, 1902.

Deissmann, A., Die neutestamentliche Formel "In Christo Jesu", von G.A.
   Deissmann. Marburg, 1892.

Dieterich, Untersuchungen zur Geschichte der griechischen Sprache, von
   der hellenistischen Zeit bis zum 10 Jahrhundert Chr., Leipzig,
   1898. (Byz. Archiv I).

Driver, G., The Original Language of the Fourth Gospel, a criticism of
   Dr. Burney's thesis. Reprinted from the Jewish Guardian, Jan.
   5 and 12, 1923.

Eissfeldt, O., Einleitung in das Alte Testament, von Otto Eissfeldt.
   2 Aufl. Tübingen, 1956.

Expository Times, edited by J. Hastings, afterward by A.W. and E. Hastings. Edinburgh, 1880ff.

Gregg, J.A.F., The Wisdom of Solomon in the revised version with introduction and notes, by J.A.F.Gregg. (Cambridge Bible) Cambridge, 1909.

Hawkins, J.C., Horae Synopticae, by J.C.Hawkins. 2nd ed. Oxford, 1909.

Howard, W.F., *A Grammar of New Testament Greek*, by J.H. Moulton, and W.F.Howard. Vol. ii- Accidence and Word-Formation with an appendix on Semitisms in the New Testament. Edinburgh, 1929.

Jannaris, A.N., *An Historical Greek Grammar*, by A.N.Jannaris. London, 1897.

Journal of Biblical Literature- New Haven, 1881ff.

Journal of Theological Studies- Oxford, 1900ff.

Lagrange, J., *Evangile selon Saint Marc*, par J. Lagrange. Et.Bibl. Paris, 1920.

Lightfoot, J.B., *Saint Paul's Epistle to the Philippians*, a revised text with introduction, notes, and dissertations, by J.B. Lightfoot. London, 1879.

Meisterhans, K., *Grammatik der Attischen Inschriften*. Dritte vermehrte und verbesserte Aufl. von Eduard Schwyzer. Berlin, 1900.

Moulton, J.H., *A Grammar of New Testament Greek*, by J.H.Moulton. Vol.i, Prolegomena. 2nd ed. Edinburgh, 1906.

Moulton and Milligan, *The Vocabulary of the Greek Testament* illustrated from the Papyri and other (non-literary) sources. London, 1914- 1929.

Olsson, Bror, *Papyrusbriefe aus der frühesten Römerzeit*. Uppsala, 1925.

Philologien Studien, Katholieke Universitat te Leuve.

Radermacher, L., *Neutestamentliche Grammatik*. Das Griechisch des NT in Zusammenhang mit der Volkssprache. Tübingen, 1911.

Sharp, D.S., *Epictetus and the New Testament*, by D.S.Sharp. London, 1914.

Swete, H.B., *The Gospel according to St. Mark*; the Greek text with introduction, notes, and indices. London, 1909.

Taylor, V., *The Gospel according to St. Mark*, by Vincent Taylor. London, 1952.

Thackeray, H.St.J., *A Grammar of the Old Testament in Greek* according to the Septuagint; Introduction, Orthography and Accidence, by Henry St.John Thackeray. Cambridge, 1909.

Torrey, C.C., *Ezra Studies*, by C.C.Torrey. Chicago, 1910.

Viteau, *Etude sur le Grec du NT compare avec lui des Septante*. Sujet, Complement et Attribut. Paris, 1897.

Winer, G.B., *A Treatise on the Grammar of NT Greek*, by G.B.Winer, translated from the German by W.F.Moulton. 9th Eng. ed. Edinburgh, 1882.

A LIST OF ABBREVIATIONS

GNTG- Blass-Debrunner, Grammatik des neutest. Griechisch. 5 Aufl.
bearbeitet von A. Debrunner. Gottingen, 1921.

GNTGE- A Grammar of New Testament Greek by Friedrich Blass. Tr. by
Henry St.J. Thackeray. London, 1898.

AG- Kühner-Gerth, Ausfuhrliche Grammatik der griech. Sprache. II Teil:
Satzlehre. 3 Aufl. von B. Gerth (2 Bde.) Hannover und
Leipzig, 1898-1904.

GGP- Mayser, E., Grammatik der griechischen Papyri aus der Ptolmäerzeit.
Band II: Satzlehre. i- Berlin und Leipzig, 1926; ii, iii-
Berlin und Leipzig, 1934.

BDB- Brown, Driver and Briggs, A Hebrew and English Lexicon of the Old
Testament, by Francis Brown, S.R.Driver, and Charles A.
Briggs. Boston and New York, 1907.

G-K- Gesenius-Kautzsch, Gesenius' Hebrew Grammar, ed. by E. Kautzsch.
Eng. tr. Collins and Cowley. Oxford, 1910.

www.ingramcontent.com/pod-product-compliance
Lightning Source LLC
Chambersburg PA
CBHW030939090426
42737CB00007B/476